Start Your Own

GRAPHIC DESIGN BUSINESS

Additional titles in *Entrepreneur's **Startup Series***

Start Your Own

Entrepreneur MAGAZINE'S

start up

Start Your Own

GRAPHIC DESIGN BUSINESS

Your Step-by-Step Guide to Success

Entrepreneur Press and George Sheldon

Ep
Entrepreneur Press

Jere L. Calmes, Publisher
Managing Editor: Marla Markman
Cover Design: Beth Hansen-Winter
Production and Composition: Eliot House Productions

This publication is designed to provide accurate and authoritative information in regard
to the subject matter covered. It is sold with the understanding that the publisher is not
engaged in rendering legal, accounting or other professional services. If legal advice or
other expert assistance is required, the services of a competent professional person
should be sought.

Library of Congress Cataloging-in-Publication Data
    Sheldon, George.
        Start your own graphic design business/by Entrepreneur Press and George Sheldon.
            p.   cm.   —(Startup series)
        ISBN-13: 978-1-59918-163-9 (alk. paper)
            1. Commercial art—Marketing. 2. Graphic arts—Marketing. 3. Entrepreneurship—
        Handbooks, manuals, etc. 4. New business enterprises—Handbooks, manuals, etc.
        5. Small business—Handbooks, manuals, etc. I. Title.
    NC1001.S43 2008
    741.6068'8—dc22   2007040617

Printed in Canada

13 12 11 10 09   10 9 8 7 6 5 4 3 2

Contents

▲

Preface

Graphic designer. It kind of sounds like someone in charge, right? From the initial idea, the designer starts the work and poof, magically a great new piece has been created. From a scribble on a napkin—all great designs start on coffee-stained napkins, don't they?—a new logo is born. Within months, that logo starts appearing everywhere—from business cards to billboards. It's on packages, labels, reports, boxes, brochures, catalogs, and even on those shirts the company's employees wear.

It's great to be a graphic designer. It's challenging and creative work. And it's ever-changing.

It is hard to think of any other creative profession that has undergone more massive changes in recent years than graphic art and design. Writers, for example, have abandoned their typewriters for word processors, but many successful writers and authors use word processing software that is a decade old. They do not need the most recent updates in either hardware or software. With what others would consider an outdated or legacy computer, the writer churns out manuscript after manuscript.

Using outdated equipment is not an option for graphic artists and designers. They may still use traditional methods to create some art. For example, they might draw an illustration with black ink and a pen, the same method used for decades. But just about everything else has changed in the last 30 years.

Graphic designers now use computers to produce their work, but not just any old computer. Because of their need for extensive computer graphics, today's designers often need and use the latest, most advanced technology to produce their work. Animation, for example, once drawn one picture frame at a time by an artist, is now totally automated. Today's animation is created on computer screens. Those computers that produce animation sequences are not like the machines that only need to drive word processing software. The software has tremendous capability, but it also requires more from the hardware: extra memory, substantial disk space, and faster processors.

The graphic artists and designers that use these kinds of powerful computers and software to create their work must become experts on their machines. They must master and develop a high level of expertise with their software. Those that do are quick to find work, either as an employee or a freelance graphic artist. Their services are worth money—and plenty of companies, organizations, associations, and businesses are willing to pay for it.

Yes, the world of a graphic designer has changed, and shows no signs of slowing down. It's an exciting—and profitable time—to be a graphic artist or designer. A skilled graphic designer with sound credentials and strong interpersonal skills can easily earn $40,000 to $60,000 per year or more as an employee or an independent contractor. If that same graphic designer understands the basics of starting and running a business, he or she will find the opportunities presented by owning a graphic design agency virtually limitless.

Employment and Jobs

A recent trade industry report found that U.S. design salaries are up, and demand remains steady. Because of the varied names and descriptions of design jobs, it is difficult to make exact comparisons.

According to the AIGA (American Institute of Graphic Arts)/Aquent 2007 survey, "margins are tighter and clients are contracting for work against smaller budgets." However, the overall trend is still positive, with signs that American businesses are recognizing the value of innovative design in promoting themselves internationally. In 2007, the design salaries survey reported an upward trend in graphic designers' earnings. For 2006, salaries were slightly down, but the trend is still looking good from a workload point of view. "As expected, art directors and senior designers earn considerably more than junior designers," the AIGA website reported. "Freelance or self-employed designers tended to earn the equivalent of a senior designer's salary."

From a regional point of view, substantial wage differences remain. For example, graphic designers in New York City, San Francisco, Los Angeles, and Atlanta were near the top of the salary pile. Designers working in Denver, Dallas, and Philadelphia earned at the lower end of the income ladder.

The opportunities for freelance graphic artists and designers are growing at a rapid rate. Graphic designers work on a wide array of projects and media. With the never-ending development of new electronic media and electronic communication, graphic designers capable of producing digital images will certainly remain in demand.

Whether you want to start a part-time graphic design business, or a one-person full-time operation, or build a substantial company with a full stable of graphic designers and trainees to work with you, this book is for you. Regardless of the type of graphic design business you want to start, I recommend that you read every chapter in this book. Most of the information applies to all sizes and types of graphic design operations, and the information is interrelated.

I'll start with an overview of the industry, looking at the market, who is using graphic designers and why, and what services graphic designers are offering. Then I'll go through the step-by-step process of setting up and running your new venture. You'll learn about basic requirements and startup costs, day-to-day operations, and what to do when things don't go according to plan. You'll gain a solid understanding of the sales and marketing process, as well as how to track and manage the financial side of your business. Throughout the book, you'll hear from industry experts as well as graphic designers who are eager to share what they've learned.

What this book won't do is teach you how to be a graphic designer. There are hundreds of organizations and schools that provide courses or study programs on graphic design, desktop publishing, and other related topics. Seek out the best of those courses to build your own professional knowledge base and credentials. This book focuses on the business side of graphic design, giving you the fundamental information you need to start and build the company you want to own.

You also need to know from the start that most graphic designers do not find the business side of their operations as enjoyable as they do working with clients. You'll probably feel the same way, and that's fine. But you must give the business functions (administration, marketing, financial management, etc.) the attention they need, or you won't have a business for long.

However, don't think "business" is necessarily synonymous with drudgery. Business should be fun as well as profitable, so I've designed this book to be logical, informative, and entertaining. Take the time to sit back and relax now, because once your graphic design business is up and running, you're going to be a very busy person.

The Right
Stuff

Graphic designers, or graphic artists, create, produce, or generate graphics and designs to meet the specific commercial or promotional needs of their employers or clients. They develop and make the designs for packaging, displays, or logos.

The definition of graphic designer has blurred in recent years. Today, graphic designers work in multimedia, graphic design, visual communication, advertising, animation, web development, and so on. They often create, maintain, and expand websites as another aspect of the business.

Graphic designers use a variety of mediums to achieve a variety of artistic or decorative effects. As artists, today's designer may use traditional methods, such as ink, paint, or charcoal on paper, to create a design. However, the majority use computers to create their designs.

Several decades ago, the graphic designer's portfolio was usually a large black book or oversized binder. The graphic designers carried samples of their best printed pieces to show prospective clients or employers their previous work. Over the last 20 years, however, the portfolios of most graphic designers have become digitized. Their portfolios are now accessed via a website on the internet, a CD, or a DVD.

What Is Graphic Design?

Graphic design is visual problem solving. Using text and graphical elements, a specific message is conveyed. The goal of a graphic designer is to create designs and work that is pleasing to the eye. In addition, the finished piece should get the attention of its viewer.

But what you create can't just look cool. Your designs have to work as well. For example, consider a restaurant menu. If poorly arranged, customers cannot find appetizers, and the restaurant's sales of these items will diminish. If the beverage section cannot not be located or the prices are unreadable, patrons are not likely to order them. But a great design can entice the restaurant customer to order. As you can see from this simple example, a good design can increase orders and sales (and profits), or it can hamper sales and diminish the likelihood of profitability.

Graphic design is the art and process of combining text and graphics. The goal is to communicate an effective and efficient message with the design of text, logos, graphics, newsletters, brochures, posters, photos, images, signs, or any other kind of visual communication.

Employment Outlook

Among the five design occupations the Bureau of Labor Statistics (BLS) describes in the *Occupational Outlook Handbook 2006–07*, graphic designers are expected to have the most new jobs through 2014. However, job seekers should

Other Names of Graphic Designers

Graphic designer is just one name used to describe the person that creates graphic designs. Other terms include:

- ○ Brand identity developer
- ○ Content developer
- ○ Desktop publisher
- ○ Graphic artist
- ○ Illustrator
- ○ Interface designer
- ○ Layout artist
- ○ Logo designer
- ○ Multimedia developer
- ○ Visual image developer
- ○ Web designer

In addition to these hands-on positions, there are also graphic designers who become managers and supervise the production of the design work. These graphic art managers, who are experienced graphic designers, serve in management roles. Some of their titles are:

- ○ Creative director
- ○ Art director
- ○ Art production manager

anticipate keen competition for available positions. The BLS believes the competition will be intense because the work is attractive to many people. "Graphic designers with website design and animation experience will have the best opportunities," the BLS says.

The BLS reports that a bachelor's degree is required for most entry-level positions. The job applicant will need some sort of certificate or degree to land a job as a graphic designer in specialized areas such as multimedia or graphic design. However, an associate degree may be sufficient for technical positions. Other sources indicate that an advanced degree is not always necessary for employment. Experience and an extensive portfolio can often open the doors to employment, as either a regular employee or a freelancer.

Fun Fact

The late Phil Hartman, who became famous for his TV and movie comedy, worked as a graphic designer. He created the logo for Crosby, Stills, Nash, and Young.

The Nature of the Work

Graphic designers (or graphic artists) plan, prepare, and create visual solutions to a wide range of communications issues. Designers decide the most effective way of delivering a message in various media. They work in print, electronic, and film media, using a variety of methods, such as color, type, illustration, photography, animation, and various print and layout techniques.

Graphic designers develop the final layout and production design of magazines, newspapers, journals, corporate reports, and other documents and publications. They produce all types of communications. They also create promotional displays, packaging, and marketing brochures for products and services, design distinctive logos for products and businesses, and develop signs.

> **Bright Idea**
> Graphic designers also create signage systems, called *environmental graphics*. These systems are used for both business and government.

There are an increasing number of graphic designers that work with developing material for the internet. Web pages, interactive media, and multimedia projects are now routine work for graphic designers. Rather than rely on a computer programmer to design the layout or look and feel of a website, a graphic artist creates the site.

Graphic designers also may produce the openings, including the credits that appear before and after audio-visual television shows, films, and movies.

Graphic artists develop new graphic designs by determining the needs of the client, the message the design should portray, and its desired appeal to customers or users. They consider various factors in planning and executing designs for the intended audience, and gather relevant information by conducting and attending meetings with clients and creative directors. Graphic artists also routinely conduct their own research to help create the final designs.

As part of their work, graphic designers routinely prepare sketches or layouts—by hand or with the aid of a computer—to illustrate their vision for the final design. Graphic artists select colors, sound, artwork, photography, animation, style of type, and other visual elements for their conceptual designs.

Designers also select the size and arrangement of the different elements on the page, product, film, or computer screen. They create graphs and charts from data for use in a wide variety of publications. Graphic designers consult with copywriters about the text that accompanies the visual part of the design.

When their design is complete, graphic artists submit it to their clients or art directors for final approval. For some graphic artists, their work is completed at this point. Others may work with commercial printers by selecting the type of paper and ink and reviewing the proofs for errors before final publication.

Computerization and Automation

Today's graphic artists do everything that yesterday's paste-up artists (and others—such as typesetters and camera workers) did. There is much more to current graphic arts jobs than ever before. It is much more technical and far less mechanical.

Graphic artists use a wide variety of graphics and layout computer software. The days of using mechanical paste-up, or actually assembling type and illustration images onto boards with glue or wax to produce finished pages for graphic projects, are gone.

Today's graphic artists work on computers to set type. They are highly trained and proficient in typography. Typesetters that sent finished type to paste-up artists are gone. So are the paste-up artists. This work has been automated by computerization.

The graphic artists of today also manipulate photographic and other digital images as part of their regular work. In the past, other technicians or artistic specialists working with large cameras did that image work. Now the graphic artists must make sure images print properly, look nice, and are appealing to the eye. Yesterday's paste-up artists did little of this.

The computer programs that graphic artists use to create web pages or other interactive media designs are expanding and offer new features and capabilities. For example, computer-created animation is standard today. Gone are the days when artists would draw each film frame on a clear piece of plastic, commonly called a *cell*. Today's computer software programs allow ease and flexibility in exploring a greater number of design alternatives. Combined with far less expensive computer hardware, the graphic artist's computer tools reduce both design costs and the time it takes to deliver a product or message to market.

> ### Fun Fact
> Although it was called *paste-up*, graphic artists did not actually use paste, which was found to be unacceptable and unworkable. They actually used wax to place and slide type and graphic elements on the boards.

Other Considerations

Graphic artists sometimes supervise assistants that help work on parts of a project. Graphic artists who run their own businesses also may devote a considerable amount of their work time in developing new business contacts, evaluating equipment and space needs, and performing general and routine administrative duties. The need for up-to-date computers (both hardware and software) is an ongoing consideration for graphic artists.

Working Conditions

According to the Bureau of Labor Statistics, working conditions and the places of employment for graphic artists vary: "Graphic designers employed by large advertising, publishing, or design firms generally work regular hours in well-lighted and comfortable settings. Designers in smaller design consulting firms or those who freelance generally work on a contract, or job, basis. They frequently adjust their workday to suit their clients' schedules and deadlines. Consultants and self-employed designers tend to work longer hours and in smaller, more congested environments."

Graphic artists transact business in their own offices or studios or in clients' offices. Those who are paid by the assignment often find themselves under pressure to please clients and to find new ones in order to maintain a steady income.

All designers—no matter how they are compensated or where they work—face frustration when their designs are rejected. Sometimes, their work is not as creative as they wish and becomes more routine as they work on larger projects.

Graphic designers may work under pressure to get work done. This could mean working evenings or weekends to meet production schedules. This is especially true in the printing and publishing industries where deadlines are routinely shorter and more frequent.

Training and Other Qualifications

The Bureau of Labor Statistics says a bachelor's degree is required for most entry-level and advanced graphic design positions, although it adds that some entry-level technical positions may only require an associate degree. In addition to training in graphic design, job applicants must possess creativity and communication and problem-solving skills. Graphic designers also need to be familiar and proficient with the latest computer graphics and design software. A good portfolio—a representative collection of examples of a graphic artist's best work—often is the deciding factor in getting a job.

The Bureau of Labor Statistics described the formal education options:

Bachelor's of fine arts degree programs in graphic design are offered at many colleges, universities, and private design schools. The curriculum includes studio art, principles of design, computerized design, commercial graphics production, printing techniques, and website design. In addition to design courses, a liberal arts education or a program that includes courses in art history, writing, psychology, sociology, foreign languages and cultural studies, marketing, and business are useful in helping designers work effectively with the content of their work. Graphic designers must effectively communicate complex subjects to a variety of audiences. Increasingly, clients rely on graphic designers to develop the content and the context of the message in addition to performing technical layout work.

Some graphic artists seek and find employment without any formal education. Many have on-the-job experience, often gained without any previous particular desire to enter the profession. Some were hired for other jobs, and because of an employer's need, are assigned graphic design work tasks. This is quite common in the industry. For example, a person might be employed as an administrative assistant, but work assignments may shift from clerical support to typical desktop publishing work. After learning software and gaining meaningful work experience, the person then seeks employment requiring graphic design skills.

Art and design education is always desirable. This educational foundation can help throughout a graphic designer's career.

The Bureau of Labor Statistics says,

Associate degrees and certificates in graphic design also are available from two- and three-year professional schools. These programs usually focus on the technical aspects of graphic design and include very few liberal arts courses. Graduates of two-year programs normally qualify as assistants to graphic designers or for positions requiring technical skills only. Individuals who wish to pursue a career in graphic design—and who already possess a bachelor's degree in another field—can complete a two-year or three-year program in graphic design to learn the technical requirements.

The National Association of Schools of Art and Design accredits about 250 postsecondary institutions with programs in art and design. Most of these schools award a degree in graphic design. Many schools do not allow formal entry into a bachelor's degree program until a student has successfully finished a year of basic art and design courses. Applicants may be required to submit sketches and other examples of their artistic ability.

Employers expect graphic designers and graphic artist to be familiar and proficient with computer graphics and design software. Graphic designers must continually keep up to date with the latest development of updated software, usually either on their own or through software training programs.

Other Skills

Graphic designers must be creative. They need to be able to communicate their ideas in writing, visually, and verbally. And because consumer tastes change quickly, graphic artists and designers must be well-read, open to new ideas and influences, and quick to react to changing trends.

Problem-solving skills, paying attention to details, and the ability to work independently and under pressure also are important traits for the graphic artist. Graphic artists and designers need self-discipline to start projects on their own, to budget their time, and to meet deadlines and production schedules. Good business sense and sales ability also are important, especially for those who freelance or run their own graphic designer business.

In the beginning of their careers, graphic designers usually receive on-the-job training. It is here where most graphic designers develop a specialization. They need about one to three years of training and experience before they can advance to higher-level positions. Their new skills developed with a specialized area of graphic design often determine their career paths.

Experienced graphic designers in large design firms may advance to chief designer, art or creative director, or other supervisory positions. Some graphic artists or designers leave the occupation to become teachers in design schools or in colleges and universities. It is common for many faculty members to consult privately or operate small design studios as freelancers to complement their classroom activities. Using their specialized skills, some experienced designers open their own firms. Others choose to specialize in one area of graphic design.

Employment Opportunities

According to the Bureau of Labor Statistics, graphic designers held about 228,000 jobs in 2004. About seven out of ten were wage and salary designers. Most worked in

- specialized design services,
- advertising and related services,
- printing and related support activities, and
- newspaper, periodical, book, and directory companies.

Other graphic designers produce computer graphics for computer systems design firms or motion picture production firms. A small number of graphic designers work in engineering services or for management, scientific, and technical consulting firms. The BLS reported that about three out of ten designers were self-employed. Many do freelance work—full time or part time—in addition to holding a salaried job in design or in other occupations.

Future Job Outlook

The BLS says that "the employment of graphic designers is expected to grow about as fast as average for all occupations through the year 2014, as demand for graphic design continues to increase from advertisers, publishers, and computer design firms. Among the five different design occupations, graphic designers will have the most new jobs. However, graphic designers are expected to face keen competition for available positions. Many talented individuals are attracted to careers as graphic designers. Individuals with a bachelor's degree and knowledge of computer design software, particularly those with website design and animation experience, will have the best opportunities."

The opportunities for graphic artists and designers "should increase because of the rapidly expanding market for web-based information and expansion of the video entertainment market, including television, movies, video, and made-for-internet outlets. Graphic designers with website design and animation experience will especially be needed as demand for design projects increases for interactive media—websites, video games, cellular telephones, personal digital assistants (PDAs), and other technology. Demand for graphic designers also will increase as advertising firms create print and web marketing and promotional materials for a growing number of products and services."

There has been a trend to outsource some design work. Based on information from the BLS, in recent years, some computer, printing, and publishing firms have outsourced basic layout and design work to design firms overseas. This trend is expected to continue. It could have a negative impact on employment growth for lower level, technical graphic design workers.

The good news is that most higher-level graphic design jobs are expected to remain in the U.S. Those high-level jobs will focus on developing in-depth communication strategies, called *strategic design*, for clients and firms in order for them to gain competitive advantages in the market. The BLS says that strategic design work requires close proximity to the consumer in order to identify and target their needs and interests. It also says that graphic designers with a broad liberal arts education and experience in marketing and business management will be best suited for these positions.

Earnings

According to the BLS, median annual earnings for graphic designers were $38,030 in May 2004. The lowest 10 percent earned less than $23,220. The middle 50 percent earned between $29,360 and $50,840, and the highest 10 percent earned more than $65,940.

Median annual earnings in the industries employing the largest numbers of graphic designers were:

- Architectural, engineering, and related services: $42,740
- Specialized design services: $41,620

- Advertising and related services: $40,010
- Printing and related support activities: $32,830
- Newspaper, periodical, book, and directory publishers: $32,390

The American Institute of Graphic Arts reported 2005 median annual total cash compensation for graphic designers according to level of responsibility. Entry-level designers earned a median salary of $32,000 in 2005, while staff-level graphic designers earned $42,500. Senior designers, who may supervise junior staff or have some decision-making authority that reflects their knowledge of graphic design, earned $56,000. Solo designers, who freelanced or worked under contract to another company, reported median earnings of $60,000. Design directors, the creative heads of design firms or in-house corporate design departments, earned $90,000. Graphic designers with ownership or partnership interests in a firm or who were principals of the firm in some other capacity earned $100,000.

Related Occupations

The term *graphic designer* has become a generalized description of people who work with computers to create art or design. There are many other associated jobs or occupations closely associated with graphic designers that use graphic art computerization skills to create their work. They include

- artists and related workers,
- commercial and industrial designers,
- fashion designers,
- floral designers,
- interior designers,
- computer software engineers,
- drafters, and
- desktop publishers.

Other occupations involved in the design, layout, and copy of publications include those working in advertising, marketing, promotions, and public relations. Sales managers and marketing managers often work closely with graphic artists and designers. Photographers, writers, editors, printers, and prepress technicians also often work with graphic artists and designers.

2

Freelancing Graphic Designers
Running the Business

You doodle, draw, and create. Most likely, you have advanced graphic design skills. You have received accolades for your work. Yet, you want more. You want the independence of being your own boss, of operating your own business, and of making more money. The answer is simple: set up your own graphic design business.

But are you ready to operate your own business? Do you have the skills to operate the business? Have you determined what you will—and won't—do as a graphic designer? All of these questions are important as you plan your own graphic design business.

Freelance Graphic Designers

Graphic art and design appeals to many people. Perhaps it is the challenge of the work, the intrigue of working with graphics on a computer, or bottled-up artistic creativity. Whatever it is, many people are interested in the profession and a career path as a graphic designer.

There are two basic paths for graphic design work: salaried employment or self-employment. This book is not about teaching how to become a graphic designer, but rather it is about how to operate a graphic design business. As a graphic designer, you will always have something new to learn or another area or media to work. The profession is dynamic and evolving.

For those who choose the path of self-employment, one option you always have is salaried work. Many graphic artists leave freelancing because they are offered full-time or part-time jobs. There is come-and-go within the workforce. People take jobs and then exit when projects are completed, or the work grows stale or uninspiring. There's nothing wrong with this. It's part of the graphic arts industry.

This book, however, is not about how to find a job as a graphic artist or designer. It's about how to start, grow, and thrive with your own graphic design business. If you want a job as a graphic artist, that's fine and noble work. Prepare a resume and a great portfolio, and start searching the want-ads for an employer.

For those who choose self-employment as a freelance graphic designer, you'll spend a considerable amount of your time looking for clients and projects. Depending on the type of graphic artwork you do, you may need many clients or just a limited number. You might be working on hundreds of projects a year or just a few.

Freelance Graphic Designer Work

In today's world, freelance graphic designers work on all kinds of projects. Graphic designers are called upon not only for printed work, such as boxes, reports, brochures, and books) but also all forms of electronic media. This field is forever expanding, especially as new technology is developed and released to consumers. For example, consider cell phone technology. Now downloading to a cell phone is the latest craze. It is the graphic designer who will design the graphics, art, and text messages that consumers see on their tiny cell phone screens. A few years ago, this technology and work for a graphic designer did not exist. Now this area is becoming common work.

This simple example also demonstrates one of the challenges of graphic artists and designers. While they may have a natural flair and eye for good graphic design, they must keep learning the latest technology and the best way to make their designs look good while using it. And they must learn how to create designs within the narrow specifications required by each new technology product.

Freelance graphic designers work in various media for clients. Because the field is so wide and expanding, it is difficult to list every sort of project a freelance graphic designer might be called upon to complete. A simple rule is that if it involves any kind of graphical user interface (GUI), a graphic designer will be involved in the creation and maintenance of the product throughout the project.

Graphic designers use all kinds of tools and products to create their final presentations. Consider a graphic designer working at a daily newspaper. One day, that designer might be asked to create graphical charts to illustrate a news story about government spending and the budget. The next day, the graphic designer might be working on the design and layout of an advertising supplement that will be included in a future edition of the newspaper. Then there are other related projects, such as special advertising rate sheets to be distributed to potential advertisers. The graphic designer might be asked to assist in enhancing digital photographs or work on a special layout of a large feature in the paper. There could be news pages that need to be laid out and then posted to the newspaper's website. And, of course, there are the never-ending flow of advertisements. Advertisements are how the newspaper makes its money, and many advertisers request help in preparing their advertisements. Depending on the size of the newspaper, the graphic design staff size, and the experience of the graphic designer, some artists may only work on advertisements. After gaining more experience, the graphic designer may be assigned to other work. But as you can see from this general example, the work can vary greatly.

Desktop Publishing

In the mid-1980s, the term *desktop publishing* was created. Combining both a personal computer and page layout software, computer users were able to create publication-ready documents on a personal computer for either large-scale publishing or small-scale, economical laser printers. The ability to create WYSIWYG (pronounced wizzy-wig, it stands for What You See Is What You Get) page layouts on screen and then print pages at crisp 300 dots per inch (dpi) resolution was revolutionary for both the typesetting industry and the personal computer industry.

There was a problem, however. Untrained computer users often used this early software. The results of their work were often horrendous. They created terrible looking layouts. However, some were able to realize truly professional results.

As desktop publishing evolved, computer users created documents with Adobe PageMaker, Ventura Publisher, or Quark Express. Small jobs requiring a few copies of a publication were printed on a local laser printer. For larger jobs, a computer file was sent to a commercial printer for high-volume printing. As laser printers became more affordable, word processors also became more sophisticated. High-end desktop publishing software had to compete with products like Microsoft Word and WordPerfect.

The term desktop publishing evolved, too. It is now commonly used to describe page layout skills. The skills, hardware, and software are not limited to paper, reports, and books. The same skills and software are now routinely used to create graphics for point-of-sale displays, promotional items, trade show exhibits, retail package designs, and outdoor signs.

The term desktop publishing is muddled and sometimes confusing. Many people claim to know how to "desktop publish," but their skill level may be quite limited. They may only know how to place a graphic in a word processor document. There are also those who possess high-level skills, gained from a college education and years of experience. Desktop publishing skills range from technical skills such as prepress production and computer programming to creative skills such as communication design and graphic image development. The high-level skills are what are in demand by design agencies.

> **Fun Fact**
> Desktop publishing is attributed to Aldus Corporation founder Paul Brainerd. He needed a marketing catch-phrase to describe the small size and affordability of his products in contrast to the quite expensive commercial phototypesetting equipment.

> **Beware!**
> Because desktop publishing has become a fuzzy term, be careful in using it in marketing your freelance graphic design business. Many untrained, unskilled people think they can produce great results or be their own desktop publisher. You should present yourself in the marketplace with skill levels beyond those that most people today think of as desktop publishing.

Specialization versus Generalization

As you consider your transition into working as a freelance graphic designer, one of the main considerations is what services you will offer and what you won't do. As a new business operation, your tendency is likely to say that you'll do anything. It is always difficult to turn down work, especially when you need it for income.

However, trying to be a graphic designer to everyone doesn't make sense. Because the field of graphic design encompasses such a wide arena, you are better to specialize in the areas that you know best. Consider these five points as you determine what services you will offer to clients:

1. *Never take on work for which you cannot provide "thrilled" results.* You want your clients to be thrilled with whatever you produce. Producing mediocre work is not a good plan to build your business. You don't want your clients to say your work or designs are "OK." You want them to be excited about the final product.

2. *Pass on work that will take you too long to produce because of lack of experience.* For example, you might be asked to produce animation, but have never done any in the past. It may take you 80 hours to do what is a five-hour job.

3. *Don't look for work that will cost you too much to produce.* For example, you might find a job that will pay $500, but for you to do the work requires new software and another piece of computer hardware that costs $2,000. It doesn't make sense to take on this kind of work.

4. *Seek work that you can do quickly and economically.* Because you have some experience as a graphic designer, seek work in the areas where you know what you are doing.

5. *You want projects and work that will make your portfolio look great.* Don't go into any freelance assignment that you can't use as part of your portfolio when finished.

> **Tip...**
>
> **Smart Tip**
> Avoid any image or message that paints you as an "I do anything" graphic designer. Rather than offering yourself as generalist, position yourself as a specialist and an expert.

In essence, it only makes sense to specialize in graphic design areas that you know. After your business is established, you can work toward expanding into other areas, if you want to do so. But in the beginning, be the best you can in your areas of expertise. If you are a book designer, seek business only in that area. If you are an expert at advertising layout, find clients that need that kind of work. You are far more likely to find success working as a freelance graphic designer by being a specialist.

The Pleasure of the Work

As a freelance graphic designer, your work should be satisfying and pleasurable. Don't take on work that is likely to bore you or not push your creativity factor. For example, you might be offered a job to build a printer parts catalog by a water pump manufacturer. For some, this type of work is exciting. Extracting data from a database, adding images, and making them look good on a printed page is challenging and exciting work. For others, trying to make a gasket or valve look good is excruciating and exasperating.

Your work as a graphic designer should provide you pleasure and satisfaction. That's the reason you got into graphic design in the first place. As a graphic artist, there is always a creative factor. You should do whatever it takes to keep those creative juices flowing. Working on projects that provide little or no satisfaction is just not smart for the active freelance graphic designer.

Mary Cronin, a freelance graphic designer from Ann Arbor, Michigan, lists three reasons why she enjoys being a freelancer. "First, the flexibility. If I want to take a walk to clear my head in the middle of the day I can do that without having to punch in or out. If I need to take time off to attend to a family crises, I don't have to ask permission of anyone. And I can take a vacation whenever I want. I also can wear what I want to work and don't have to invest in expensive corporate clothes. Second, not having to deal with office/corporate politics or be at the mercy of poor management. Third, developing my own relationships with clients."

Cronin, who maintains a website at www.marycronindesign.com, has been a self-employed graphic designer for 12 years. When she started 12 years ago, "I didn't expect how little some clients value design. Getting people to understand the benefits you can provide is an ongoing education process. I find this mostly with people who are starting a new business. They don't realize how important a well-designed logo, ad campaign, or website is to getting their business's message across. It is an investment in their business and it takes time and money to do it correctly and well."

Running the Freelance Business

Operating a business is part of the challenge of being a freelance graphic artist. In addition to being creative and producing work, you must also operate a business. This requires an additional skill set. The good news is that you can learn to do what is necessary to be a successful entrepreneur.

Much of what you will need to do is straightforward, and certainly less creative than producing designs and art. There are legal requirements and responsibilities. You have the added burden of finding work and clients. There are bookkeeping chores as well as purchasing responsibilities.

Where to Start

No matter what business you start, there are some basic steps that you will need to take. They include

- creating the business plan,
- determining what you want from of your business, both financially and professionally,
- choosing the organizational structure,
- determining if there is a market for a graphic design business in your area,
- obtaining financing, if necessary,
- getting the required licenses and permits,
- getting any education you need to learn more about the graphic design business,
- setting up your operation, and
- creating marketing materials to attract clients.

As a businessperson, all of these topics must be explored and decisions reached. In contrast to being an employee, when operating your own freelance graphic design business you must take all these extra steps to establish and build your operation.

When asked what basic advice he would offer someone who wants to start a graphic arts design service, graphic designer Brent Almond of Kensington, Maryland, responds, "Get a degree (don't just be some yahoo who bought software and thinks they know how to design). Beyond that, get lots of experience working with clients, either as a freelancer for other firms or working at a firm. You can always hire someone to do your books, fix your computers, etc., but it's up to you to make and keep good client relationships."

Almond, who maintains a website at www.designnut.com, offers some additional advice. "Keep in touch with other designers. Bounce ideas off of other designers who you trust and whose opinion you value. Have lunch together to swap ideas and vent about clients and other work frustrations. Keep on top of your bills and invoices!"

Based close to Washington, DC, Almond says that freelancer graphic designers should, "Make it fun! Since you can do whatever you want, keep things fun and interesting by working in different places, at different times of the day. Take special days to treat yourself (movies, day trips, long breaks in the back yard or Starbucks). But also be disciplined and treat this as a real job. Set regular hours, get up and get dressed, and keep the office in a specific place (not scattered all over the place)."

Doing What You Love

"**D**o what you love and love what you do," says graphic designer Peleg Top.

The hardest thing about starting his graphic design business was breaking into a new market. "I wanted to do music industry work and had no experience in that arena," Peleg says. "It took a few years before the work started to come in but it also took a lot of marketing and self-promotion.

But he followed his motto, and did what he loved.

Peleg Top founded his design firm in his garage in 1991. Top Design has grown to become one of Los Angeles' most prestigious design firms because of his passion for clean, simple, and sophisticated design.

With years of experience operating a graphic design business under his belt, Peleg is quick to offer specific device to those that want to follow his footsteps. "Plan and organize the business side of things," Peleg says. "And have a marketing plan in place."

When he started Top Design, simple mistakes on projects created havoc. "That cost me a lot in the beginning as I was learning how to work with vendors and how to manage a project," Peleg explains. "I quickly learned to check and double check everything that goes out the door. And by mistakes I also mean typos on projects!"

During the interview, Peleg revealed that his design agency was undergoing a dynamic change.

"We are going through a change at this time as we have recently changed our niche to focus on design for the special event industry," Peleg says. "I expect it to be a great move for our firm as we excel in this arena."

Peleg Top's web site is www.topdesign.com. His site includes downloads of his portfolio, creative brief, and now, event design planning.

The Market

One of the most important aspects of any business startup is how to get your market to know you exist. But even before you get to that point, you need to determine if there is in fact a market for the type of graphic design business you are considering. The good news is that graphic designers are in demand, although some areas are more competitive than others (driving down fees). Your market research is going to depend on what type of graphic design business you want to establish. Your areas of specialization will determine if your market is local, regional, or national. For example, if the kind of work you want to do is movie credits, you need to consider that most of that postproduction work is done in Southern California.

Once you decide on the graphic business you want to create, you need to determine where you are going to work. Then, you can research whether the market is already covered in that area. Check the Yellow Pages, do an online search, and just drive around. This is particularly true if your work is likely to be used by other businesses. Locating near an industrial or commercial park, or in a downtown business district, might make a lot of sense.

Once you determine what the type of graphic design business you want, and if there is a market you can service in a specific area, it's time to think about setting up your shop.

Designing Your
Graphic Arts
Business

Some people with small businesses would prefer to wrestle live alligators in a swamp than sit down and write their business plan. Others approach the task in a completely opposite manner. They plan every minute detail and never really get to the point of launching their business. You should (and need to) find a point somewhere in the middle.

Your freelance graphic design business should start with a written business plan. This is the first step toward success. Forcing yourself to reduce your plan to writing makes you think through the entire process. It requires you to consider what equipment you have and what you will need, how you will find and service your customers, and what your financial requirements are.

You may be the greatest of all graphic artists, but if you do not have a well-thought-out business plan, you have no plan for success as a freelance graphic designer. And without a plan for success, you have a plan for failure.

If you are excited about started a freelance graphic design business, you should be just as excited about creating your business plan. It will help you determine the type of work you will seek from customers and what your capabilities are now (and need to be) to get the work. You will use your business plan as a guide, and should refer to it often in the process of building your operation.

Think of your business plan as a dynamic, living document that needs to grow and flourish if your freelance business is to be successful. It is a road map, a quite useful tool to get you from where you are now and to where you want to be.

A well-prepared business plan is worth the time and effort it takes to prepare. It forces you to think about issues and eliminates costly, even catastrophic mistakes. Don't rely on your memory and don't start a business without a formal written plan.

According to the Small Business Administration (SBA), "Owning a business is the dream of many Americans. Starting that business converts your dreams into reality. However, there is a gap between dreams and reality. Your dreams can only be achieved with careful planning. As an entrepreneur, you will need a plan to avoid pitfalls, to achieve your goals, and to build a profitable business."

The SBA advises that your business plan have seven key components:

1. Identify your reasons
2. Self-analysis
3. Personal skills and experience
4. Finding a niche
5. Market analysis
6. Planning your startup
7. Finances

Your reasons could be that you bored with the nine-to-five routine or you want to earn a greater income. You must analyze your willingness to work longer hours, to prepare and plan, and to get along with others. You must determine your niche, and then decide how it will fit in the marketplace. The final steps are developing a startup plan and financing the start until the business is profitable.

Business plans should raise questions, and answer them. Some good questions for the freelance graphic designer include:

- What's your business idea?
- How does your idea address a need?
- What business model suits you best?
- What's so different about what you offer compared to your competition?
- How big is the current market and how big will you grow your business?
- What's your role going to be in the business?
- Who's on your team?
- Will you be hiring subcontractors or employees?
- Who will be your vendors and what work might your outsource?
- How will customers find and buy from you?
- How much will your customers pay for your graphic design work?
- How much money do you need to get started?
- How much will you make as a freelance graphic artist?
- Where's the startup money coming from?
- Do you have enough money to get started now?
- How will you measure your success?
- What are your goals for your graphic design business?
- What are your important milestones for your business?

The Business Plan Format

Bright Idea

Don't forget to include information about "when things go bad" in your business plan. What would happen if you became disabled and couldn't work because of an accident or illness? Could your graphic design business survive a disaster, such as a fire? Do you have backup and recovery plans? Could you still cover your financial responsibilities if you were unable to work for three months? You will benefit from thinking negatively and working on solutions to these kinds of problems. It will also add another perspective to your business plan.

The final format of your business plan is unimportant. There are software programs and numerous books to guide you through the process. There are many formats and styles. What the final form looks like—whether it is a simple word processing document or a complicated notebook with numerous dividers—does not matter. The content and the process of considering all the angles of starting, maintaining, marketing, and growing your business is what counts.

Keep in mind that it is OK for your business plan to be as unique and as individualized as you are. There is nothing wrong with this.

However, there are some basics that you probably want to follow. By doing so, you can address all the important issues, and in the future be able to expand your plan as needed. The ten basic elements of a freelance graphic design business plan are:

1. *Front matter.* Your cover page, table of contents, and your statement of purpose.

2. *Business description.* Your description of your freelance graphic design business. List the services you will offer and the reasons you can make your business successful. Include your goals, aspirations, and startup timetable.

3. *The industry, competition, and the market.* Your industry analysis, what the current competition is, and the current market situation.

4. *Company organization.* Your organization (the legal structure), use of vendors, consultants, professionals, and advisors to help you, and other important legal considerations, including licenses, permits, or certificates you will be required to obtain.

5. *Services and operations.* Your service offerings, how you will provide those services, and what you will charge for them. Explain your pricing strategy. You should also include your operational plan—how you will fulfill orders from your clients and customers, and how the workflow will be maintained. What is it that you can, and cannot, do for your clients?

6. *Marketing plan.* Your overview of the market and how you will find and locate a potential list of clients and customers. Your analysis of your current competition needs to be here. Your plan about how you will attract customers and grow your business should be included. Discusses your strategy and timeline for achieving all of your marketing goals. Be sure to include any new or novel ideas you have for marketing your graphic design service.

7. *Financial data.* Your capitalization. How much money do you need to start your freelance graphic design business? What equipment (hardware/software) will you need to purchase? How much will your marketing cost?

8. *Financial projections.* Your projections of income and expenses. Project not just for one year, but for the next three. Be realistic. Don't forget that you will spend more time marketing and looking for clients at the beginning, and this effort will curtail your earning power. Think too about worse case scenarios: if there is a turn in the economy or a period where you might not be able to work. Include what-if statements that address alternative approaches to any problem that may develop.

9. *Summary*. Your summary of your findings where you bring everything together and highlight the merits and pluses of your plan.

10. *Appendices*. Your supporting information includes anything that makes sense, from licensing information to sample brochures or your marketing pieces.

Don't rush the preparation of the business plan. Everyone has their own style, but it should be a process. You want to work on it, then review it, and then work on it some more. Planning on paper always makes sense.

Another area to consider is your exit strategy. Describe what you see as the ultimate destiny of your graphic design company, especially as it may affect those who finance your new business. Without you, will your business still be viable?

"Starting and managing a business takes motivation, desire and talent. It also takes research and planning," the Small Business Administration says. "Like a chess game, success in small business starts with decisive and correct opening moves. And, although initial mistakes are not fatal, it takes skill, discipline, and hard work to regain the advantage."

The Service Corps of Retired Executives (SCORE), which helps new business owners, says, "It typically takes several weeks to complete a good plan. Most of that time is spent in research and re-thinking your ideas and assumptions. But then, that's the value of the process. So make time to do the job properly. Those who do never regret the effort. And finally, be sure to keep detailed notes on your sources of information and on the assumptions underlying your financial data."

Bright Idea

Prepare your business plan as if you are presenting it to a bank board, even if you are the only one that will ever see or use it, because you are planning a one-person freelance graphic design business. The more thorough your plan, the better it will be.

Stat Fact

Business experts say that a thoroughly researched business plan is at least 25 pages long and takes over 300 hours to complete. This may seem like a lot of work for a freelance graphic design business, but a plan that is too vague won't be much good either. You should take as much time as you need to finish your complete business plan.

Choosing Your Business Forms

As you are planning your freelance graphic design business, you must choose the best form of business ownership or structure. The choice you make impacts multiple aspects of your business, such as taxes, liability, and ownership succession.

How the company is to be structured is one of the first decisions that you should make as a business owner. This decision has long-term implications. For that reason, you should consult your tax advisor, accountant, and attorney to help you select the form of ownership that is right for you. As you plan and move toward that structure, you should consider:

- Your final vision regarding the size and nature of your graphic design business
- The level of control you wish to have in the business
- The level of structure you are willing to run
- The vulnerability to lawsuits and the exposure you will have
- The tax implications and obligations of the different ownership structures
- The expected profit (or loss) of the graphic arts business
- Whether you need to reinvest earnings into the business
- Your need for access to cash out of the business for yourself

Each of these areas is a subject you need to understand fully, and you should ask the professionals you consult to explain your duties, obligations, and rights.

Sole Proprietorships

The vast majority of small businesses start out as sole proprietorships. One person, usually the individual who has day-to-day responsibilities for running the business, owns the business. In a sole proprietor business, you do everything from cashing checks to emptying the trash cans, from answering the phone to completing the work your customers give you.

Sole proprietors own all the assets of the business and receive all the profits generated by it. They also assume total responsibility for any of its liabilities or debts. In the eyes of the law and the public, you are the same as the business.

There are several advantages to setting up as a sole proprietorship. These advantages include:

- It is the easiest and least expensive form of ownership to organize.
- You have complete control of the business, and within the parameters of the law, may make decisions as you see fit.
- You receive all income generated by the business, to keep or reinvest.
- Profits from the business flow directly to your personal tax return.
- The business is easy to dissolve, if desired.

There are some disadvantages of operating as a sole proprietor. They include:

- Sole proprietors have unlimited liability. This means that you are legally responsible for all debts against the business. All of your business and personal assets are at risk.

- Sole proprietors are often at a disadvantage in raising funds and are often limited to using funds from personal savings or consumer loans.

- Sole proprietors often experience difficulty attracting high-caliber employees or those who are motivated by the opportunity to own a part of a business.

- Some employee benefits such as the owner's medical insurance premiums are not directly deductible from business income (only partially deductible as an adjustment to income).

Partnerships

In a partnership, two or more people share ownership of a single business. Like proprietorships, the law does not distinguish between the business and its owners. The partners should always have a legal agreement that sets forth how decisions will be made, profits shared, and disputes resolved. The partnership agreement should also include how future partners will be admitted to the partnership, how partners can be bought out, and what steps will be taken to dissolve the partnership, if and when it may be needed. The partners must also decide how work will be handled, how much time each partner will work, and the capital each will contribute to the startup of the partnership.

There are several advantages to forming a business partnership. They include:

- It is easy to establish; however, considerable time should be invested in developing the partnership agreement.

- Because there is more than one owner, the ability to raise funds may be increased.

- All the profits from the business flow directly through to the partners' personal tax returns.

> **Tip...**
>
> **Smart Tip**
> Although it is difficult to think about a breakup when a new business is just getting started, many partnerships split up at crisis times and when things are not going as expected. Unless there is a predefined process, there will be even greater problems should it become necessary to split apart the partnership. One area of contention is what happens to the existing customer base. Make sure you have this thought out before entering a business partnership.

- Prospective employees may be attracted to the business if given the incentive of becoming a partner.

- The business usually can benefit from partners who have complementary skills.

There are several disadvantages to forming a business partnership. They include:

- Partners are jointly and individually liable for the actions of the other partners.
- Profits must be shared with others.
- Because decisions are shared, disagreements can (and often do) occur.
- Some employee benefits are not deductible from business income on tax returns.
- The partnership may have a limited life. For example, the partnership may end upon the withdrawal or death of a partner.

Types of Partnerships

Depending on your location and state laws, you also need to discuss with your legal advisors what type of partnership that should be considered. Usually, there is a general partnership, where the partners divide responsibility for management and liability, as well as the shares of profit or loss according to their internal agreement. Equal shares are assumed unless there is a written agreement that states differently.

In many locales, there are limited partnerships and partnerships with limited liability available. Limited means that most of the partners have limited liability (to the extent of their investment) as well as limited input regarding management decisions, which generally encourages investors for short-term projects or for investing in capital assets. This form of ownership is not often used for operating service businesses. Forming a limited partnership is more complex and formal than that of a general partnership.

Another form of partnership is the joint venture. This form functions like a general partnership, but is designed for a limited period of time or a single project.

Corporations

A corporation is chartered by the state in which it is headquartered. Corporations are considered by law to be a unique entity, separate and apart from those who own it. A corporation can be taxed, it can be sued, and it can enter into contractual agreements. The owners of a corporation are its shareholders. The shareholders elect a board of directors to oversee the major policies and decisions. The corporation has a life of its own and does not dissolve when ownership changes.

There are several advantages to forming a corporation. They include:

- Shareholders have limited liability for the corporation's debts or judgments against the corporations.
- Generally, shareholders can only be held accountable for their investment of stock in the company. (Note however, that officers can be held personally liable for their actions, such as the failure to withhold and pay employment taxes.)

- A corporation can raise additional funds through the sale of stock.
- A corporation may deduct the cost of benefits it provides to officers and employees.
- It is possible to elect S corporation status if certain requirements are met. This election enables the company to be taxed similarly to a partnership.

There are several disadvantages to forming a corporation. They include:

- The process of incorporation requires more time and money than other forms of organization. In other words, it takes longer to set up a corporation and requires the use of an attorney.
- Corporations are closely monitored by federal, state, and local agencies, and as a result, you often have more paperwork to complete and file in order to comply with regulations.
- Incorporating may result in higher overall taxes. Dividends paid to shareholders are not deductible from business income, so profits can be subject to double taxation.

Subchapter S Corporations

A Subchapter S corporation is a regular corporation, but for tax purposes, it is chosen as a method to determine tax liability. By choosing to be a Subchapter S corporation, the shareholders are permitted to treat the earnings and profits as distributions and have them pass through directly to their personal tax returns.

Limited Liability Company (LLC)

The LLC is a relatively new type of business structure that is permissible in most states. It is designed to provide the limited liability features of a corporation and the tax efficiencies and operational flexibility of a partnership. Formation is more complex and formal than that of a general partnership.

The owners are members, and the duration of the LLC is usually determined when the organization's papers are filed. The time limit

Smart Tip

Tip...

The catch with a Subchapter S corporation is that the shareholder, if working for the company and if there is a profit, must pay him/herself wages that must meet standards of "reasonable compensation." This varies by geographical region as well as occupation, but the basic rule is to pay yourself what you would have to pay someone else to do your job, as long as there is enough profit. If you do not do this, the IRS can reclassify all of the earnings and profit as wages, and you will be liable for all of the payroll taxes on the total amount.

can be continued, if desired, by a vote of the members at the time of expiration. LLCs must not have more than two of the four characteristics that define corporations: Limited liability to the extent of assets, continuity of life, centralization of management, and free transferability of ownership interests.

LLCs are generally faster and easier to set up than standard corporations. Your clients may prefer to do business with an LLC because then they are doing business with your enterprise, not you personally. This avoids any claims of worker's compensation or employee status with the client.

As you can see, you have many options available as you form your freelance graphic design business. Deciding the form of ownership that best suits you should be given very careful consideration. Use your professional advisors to assist you in the process. Don't go about this yourself. Seek professional assistance to avoid any problems.

Bright Idea

Many businesses hiring freelancers today want to do business with a corporation, not a sole proprietor. The reason is that they do not want you to be considered an employee. You may be at an advantage if you are a corporation and an employee of your own corporation. This could mean that you would be hired as a corporation over an individual operating as a sole proprietor. Be sure to discuss this aspect with your tax and legal advisors.

Government Help and Forms

There is much information available about operating as one of the business forms. The Internal Revenue Service (IRS) publishes lots of relevant information. By visiting its website, you can obtain all types of information. The kinds of forms you will need are available directly from the IRS online site, www.irs.com.

Federal tax forms for sole proprietorships include:
- Form 1040: Individual Income Tax Return
- Schedule C: Profit or Loss from Business (or Schedule C-EZ)
- Schedule SE: Self-Employment Tax
- Form 1040-ES: Estimated Tax for Individuals
- Form 4562: Depreciation and Amortization
- Form 8829: Expenses for Business Use of your Home
- Employment Tax Forms

Federal tax forms for partnerships include:
- Form 1065: Partnership Return of Income

- Form 1065 K-1: Partner's Share of Income, Credit, Deductions
- Form 4562: Depreciation
- Form 1040: Individual Income Tax Return
- Schedule E: Supplemental Income and Loss
- Schedule SE: Self-Employment Tax
- Form 1040-ES: Estimated Tax for Individuals
- Employment Tax Forms

Federal tax forms for regular or C corporations include:
- Form 1120 or 1120-A: Corporation Income Tax Return
- Form 1120-W: Estimated Tax for Corporation
- Form 8109-B: Deposit Coupon
- Form 4625: Depreciation
- Employment Tax Forms
- Other forms as needed for capital gains, sale of assets, alternative minimum tax, etc.

Federal tax forms for Subchapter S corporations include:
- Form 1120S: Income Tax Return for S Corporation
- 1120S K-1: Shareholder's Share of Income, Credit, Deductions
- Form 4625: Depreciation
- Employment Tax Forms
- Form 1040: Individual Income Tax Return
- Schedule E: Supplemental Income and Loss
- Schedule SE: Self-Employment Tax
- Form 1040-ES: Estimated Tax for Individuals

State and Local Regulations and Laws

In addition to complying with the federal laws, you also need to comply with all the state and local regulations. As you are forming your freelance graphic design business, ask your professional advisors about your duties and obligations under local laws. You may need to obtain a sales tax license or other permits. You may be subject to additional regulations or laws, depending upon the type of business structure you choose.

Employment Identification Numbers

If you opt to establish your freelance graphic design business as a sole proprietor, you can use your own Social Security number when filing your business taxes. Other business forms, such as a partnership or corporation, require you to apply and get an employment identification number (EIN). Sometimes also called a taxpayer identification number (TIN), these account numbers are obtained at no cost from the IRS.

The fastest and easiest way to obtain your EIN is online at the IRS website, www.irs.gov. You can also get the EIN by completing and filing the IRS form SS-4. This form is available at any IRS office. You can also print one from the website, if you prefer.

The Final Decision

As you can see, establishing your business can be simple or complicated, depending on your legal formation. As a sole proprietor, you can open your design business today. As a corporation, it may be several weeks, if not months, before you can commence your business operations.

Although it is possible to form a corporation without an attorney, corporation law is complicated and involved. You could be making a costly mistake—and legally binding yourself to tax or other legal obligations. Because of the complexity, it is often best for you to seek advice from your legal representative in the setup of your corporation.

Learning from Other Graphic Designers

Petrula Vrontikis launched her freelance graphic design business in 1989. She offers specific advice to others who want to follow her, "Decide whether you want to freelance or make the commitment to start a business."

She adds, "Statistics are that 60 percent of graphic design businesses, started solo or in partnerships, will fail within four years. There are many reasons firms fail, but some can be anticipated at the onset and handled wisely."

Vrontikis says that if you want to operate a freelance graphic design business, "Your foundation should be a good graphic design education at one of the top schools. Get business advice from night classes or seminars before you begin. It's best to work as an employee for a couple of small- or medium-sized design offices first to see what works creatively, and business-wise . . . and what doesn't."

"Be very careful about creating partnerships. It's best to work together for a while before taking the leap," she adds. "Usually the challenge is defining each person's role, and to create a structure that lets roles change over time. If both partners want to climb mountains, there's no one tending base camp. Start with one or two large projects in an industry you are familiar with. Try to keep from working on design projects for your friends or family, even if they pay you. They are the worst clients. Ever."

"Develop decision-making and leadership skills in order to have the respect of your clients and staff. Take a course or seminar in verbal presentation skills. It will make an enormous difference in your ability to see properly your creative ideas be realized and appreciated," she says.

"Work for a company first," says Sharon Reuter. She's a freelance designer based in Baltimore, Maryland, and maintains a website at www.reuter.net. Together with her husband, she launched Reuter & Associates in 1990. "Don't start off in your own business. Learn the ropes from others and make all the contacts you can make. We have found that contacts are really valuable. Also, location doesn't matter anymore, so all the contacts we made in New York City still help us today."

Cash Flow

Most freelance graphic designers mention cash flow as a problem. "It seems you are always dealing with cash flow," says Mary Cronin of Ann Arbor, Michigan. "Not having a guaranteed steady income" was on the top of her list of the worst things about being self-employed as a graphic artist.

"Never knowing when the next project (or paycheck) will appear," is Sharon Reuter's complaint. She adds that "Estimating salary to pay quarterly taxes" can be challenging for the self-employed. "Revenue fluctuates from one year to the next so it is difficult to guess."

Your business plan should include this typical problem. You should cover how you will develop a pool of cash and how much this reserve will be. Having the ability to survive the ups and downs of cash flow as a graphic artist or designer is crucial.

Getting
Set Up

Part of the planning process is getting your work space set up so you can begin working. This is more exciting that writing a business plan or meeting with an attorney to discuss legally establishing your freelance design enterprise.

By the time you plan (and commence) the actual setup of your freelance graphic design business, you should have a pretty good idea as to what kind of work you want to do. That decision determines how you need to set up your actual work space. Obviously, if you have a partner, you need more space than if you are part-time, sole designer operation.

Some graphic artists are truly independent, working off a powerful laptop in the corner of a busy coffee shop. Others work in cubicles or open spaces in office complexes. Your decision of where and how you will work determines your overhead and profitability, and influences many of your business decisions.

Designing Your Business Name

As part of the setup process, you'll need to decide on a business name. This decision is often intertwined with the legal business entity you establish (see Chapter 3). If, for example, you opted to form a corporation, the business name is decided at that time.

If you are operating as a sole proprietor, you can operate under your own name or a fictitious name, such as

- Mary Jones, Graphic Designer,
- Jones Graphic Design, or
- Philadelphia Design.

Depending on your location and state laws, you may have to file a fictitious name certificate. After paying a fee, your business name is registered in a public file. Only you can use the name, and of course, anyone can find out who the owner of the business enterprise is.

If you incorporate, you must include the legal designation of the business as part of your enterprise name, such as

- Mary Jones, Graphic Designer, LLC,
- Jones Graphic Design, Incorporated, or
- Philadelphia Design Corporation.

Some graphic artists or designers use the street name as their business name. For example, 123 North Main might be a fictitious name of a design company located at 123 North Main Street.

> **Smart Tip** *Tip...*
>
> Your company name can be an effective marketing tool for you. The correct name can work to help you establish business, or it can mean that you will have to work much harder at marketing your design business. When picking your name, give it careful consideration.

As a graphic designer, you probably won't take too long to come up with a name for your design enterprise. You have an option to choose a specific name, or something more generic, for example, Jones Design Studio or Jones Web Design. Notice how the first example is generic and could cover all kinds of design work. The second limits your design work to websites. Consider if you want a specific name or something more generic. Whatever you choose can help or hurt your marketing efforts over the years.

Your Work Space

Your freelance graphic design business requires a work space. Depending on your business plan and what services you offer, you need a professional office space or a home office. Each choice has its advantages and disadvantages.

The Home Office

A home office allows you the freedom to work in a spare bedroom, dressed as you want, and when you want. You can work comfortably to the wee hours of the morning. There is no commute time. All the conveniences of your home are close by. The home office also creates a tax friendly situation, allowing you to deduct specific expenses.

The home office also eliminates the need to pay additional rent or increase your overhead. Many times, this is the reason why home offices are established by graphic artists. A homebased graphic design office is not a deterrent to most potential clients. It is in vogue to have and work from a home office in today's telecommunication world. Graphic artists or designers are often thought of as working from their homes.

Disadvantages of the home office include the inability to invite clients to your office to meet, little separation between work and home, and ease of goofing-off. A home office often does not work well if you have employees, and depending on the location of your home, you may not be permitted to operate a business from it. This is especially true of co-ops and condominium properties. Make sure you are allowed to operate a home business from your home early in your planning process.

Bright Idea
Because freelancers are known to work from their homes, it is not difficult to prove your legitimate use of a home office and to qualify for the home office deduction. Your goal is to comply fully with the Internal Revenue Service regulations and document the business use of your home office. You can learn more about legitimate home office deductions directly from the IRS by reading Publication 587, *Business Use of Your Home.*

Commercial Space

Renting or leasing commercial space is often something the freelance graphic designer considers. There are many factors. Office space often rents from $5 per square foot all the way up to $25 per square foot. Setting up an office away from your home increases your overhead, and costs more to maintain. The monthly cost of office space is a variable that often can have a big impact on a business' bottom line.

If you are seeking commercial space, try to find an office area that meets your business's needs without emptying your bank account. Location is important, but so are issues such as cost, usability, and condition. It is common for many businesses to get to a point where finding an outside-of-the-home of office is not a luxury, but a necessity.

Office space is often needed for several graphic designers to work together, or for meeting clients. As a graphic design business grows, it coordinating work and projects becomes a necessity.

After making the decision to lease commercial office space, the next step is to assess your company's current and future needs. Graphic designers seldom need high-end space to meet their needs.

There are often less-expensive alternatives for the graphic designer considering renting commercial office space. Often less expensive space can be transformed into an environment that stimulates creativity. As a designer, creativity is a big part of your primary business. Your work space should enhance your creativity, and not stifle it. A brightly-colored, less formal design might work as the space you need. Lofts and warehouses often work well for graphic design businesses. They have the advantage of providing inspiring space for employees as well as potential prospects and clients.

If an open and informal space is not available, consider moving into reasonably priced office space that can be broken up into different areas. Always invest more resources in meeting or conference rooms that potential clients will use. Spend less in rooms used by employees. As long as you don't give clients a tour of your space, potential buyers will assume all of your rooms are as nice as the ones they are in.

Always try to lease the best office space you can afford. That is because the work environment counts. Studies have consistently shown that employees who work in nicer office spaces are happier and more productive than employees who work in cheaper, less attractive spaces. Although you may save a few dollars, your graphic designer business may suffer if you locate in a low-rent building.

Meeting Space

A prime consideration for freelance graphic designers is the ability to meet with clients. For many design assignments, an initial meeting is crucial. Many freelancers use the client's office for meetings. This is often an easy solution although it does take time because of your need to travel. It also eliminates expensive office space, conference room furniture, and presentation equipment. A conference room can cost between $5,000 and $10,000 (or more) to furnish and set up.

If your client base does not have office space, you need another alternative meeting place. Some graphic designers use shared office space or rent the use of a conference room. Some enterprising graphic artists become creative in getting the use of a conference room. One graphic artist in Baltimore, Maryland, does a trade with a real estate office. Occupying a spare office, the artist has full use of several different sized conference rooms. In return for free use of the space, she creates the real estate office's large display ads for the Sunday newspapers.

The Space Needed

Whether you decide to establish an office in your home or in commercial space, you must consider your space requirements. Because this is where you generate your work (and your income), the work space must support this effort. In addition to allowing your creativity to flourish, the work space must be able to support the equipment you need.

Your work space must include storage for supplies. If you will be meeting with clients in your office, you will need to include a conference table and chairs, as well the ability to provide light refreshments and toilet facilities.

Your office needs a workstation where you can work as a graphic artist. You also need space to operate your business. You will have chores associated with the daily operation, from paying bills to billing customers. You will need the ability to conduct your own marketing campaigns to locate customers and work assignments. Often this is done at the same desk, so your desk will have to serve both purposes.

Don't overlook the space for the equipment you must have. These include color laser printers and scanners, and other items necessary to produce the art for your clients.

Planning the office is necessary, but it should also be fun. Don't overlook the little extras that make working in your space exciting: plants or photographs, music or posters. Whatever it is that helps you and your creativity, be sure to include it in your work space.

Your Equipment

As a working graphic designer, you probably already know what software and hardware and noncomputer supplies and materials you need. Very likely you will be using a Macintosh computer, and probably you will be using Adobe software.

The Macintosh or Mac, manufactured by Apple Inc., is the graphical king of personal computers. Originally, it was enthusiastically accepted and endorsed by the professional creative community because it used a graphical user interface (GUI) and mouse instead of the then-standard command line interface. In other words, the Mac was, and still is, a computer that uses a graphical operating system.

The various Mac models today are mainly targeted at the home, education, and creative professional markets. All current Mac models come with a pre-installed version of the latest Mac Operating System, but they can also run other operating systems, most notably Microsoft's Windows.

Bright Idea

Because you will operating a freelance graphic design business and will be using a Macintosh, you may need a Windows-based PC, too. Many business software programs (such as accounting and contact managers) are only available on Windows machines. If you have a newer Macintosh, you might also add Windows to run those programs.

Applications currently marketed by Apple Inc. include software for professional film and video editing, professional compositing and visual effects for large format film and video productions, professional music production and music post production, professional and consumer DVD encoding and authoring, professional digital photo editing and workflow management, consumer digital video and digital photo editing and management, digital music management, desktop-based database management, word processing, and high-quality presentations. Third-party vendors, most notably Adobe, produce software products for both the Mac and Windows machines.

Brent Almond, the creative graphic artist who operates www.designnut.com, reports he has the following equipment in his office:

- *Computer.* Apple G5, Epson scanner, HP LaserJet, Epson color printer, two external hard drives, Mac PowerBook
- *Other equipment.* Brother fax machine, Uniden phone, Palm Treo
- *Software.* Adobe CS2, Quark 6.5, Microsoft Office, native Mac mail, iCal, address book, Adobe Acrobat Professional 7.0, Firefox, Suitcase Fusion, Stuffit, Fetch, Photo Mechanic
- *Furniture.* Desk, bookshelves, cabinets for samples, cube bookshelf (all from IKEA), two small file cabinets in office, large file cabinet in basement for samples and client photos, office chair, two additional stools

Petrula Vrontikis equipped the Vrontikis Design Office a bit differently. "We are all Mac based and use Adobe Creative Suite software for our design work. We have Steelcase file cabinets, Rezek desks, drawers, lighting, and, of course, Aeron chairs. Because we spent so much money on the chairs, our shelves and picture frames are from IKEA," she says. "We got the office kitten for free."

Must-Haves

You must have the equipment and capability to produce the work that your clients need. Your area of specialization determines your "creative" software needs. For example, if you decide that your graphic design business will only produce low-cost logos, you may need only one piece of software to produce those logos.

This software then drives your hardware needs. If you need software capable of producing logos, you choose the software that can do the job. Then you determine if that software can be used on your hardware.

While everyone wants the latest, biggest, and best hardware, from a business standpoint you should curtail unnecessary spending and maintain a budget. Keeping cash in reserve, unless you have unlimited financial resources, makes sense. However, you also need to be able to produce what you promise to clients.

As a businessperson, you need more than just graphics software. Accounting software, such as Intuit's QuickBooks or Microsoft's Office Accounting, are helpful to track your expenses, pay bills, and manage receivables. You also need word processor and spreadsheet capabilities for various business functions.

What You Can Get Later

Balancing what you need now and what you need later is often difficult. But it makes sense to plan. You may *want* a new computer, but do you *need* it? It probably makes sense to wait until a certain milepost is achieved, such as a specific amount of sales or a particular date.

Planning your major purchases is an important part of budgeting. Set a limit on what is a small purchase. For higher-priced amounts, purchase when (and if) needed. For example, you might set a threshold of $250 and below as a small purchase. Items costing more will be purchased on a schedule, based on sales and need.

Only you can decide what you need now and what you can get later. This is part of your business plan. Most likely, you have some equipment now. Based on your financial resources and current needs, you can determine what additional equipment needs to be purchased immediately and what can be postponed.

Part of your planning is to work with hypothetical costs and expenses. To assist in this

Bright Idea

It makes no sense to purchase items or equipment you don't need now. If you are going to add a new service, perhaps animation, and need a new computer and software to provide the service, time the purchase with the service offering. If your current schedule and workload means you can't offer the service for six months, keep your money in reserve.

▲

process and planning, use the information in the Startup Expenses and Office Equipment/Supplies forms below and on the following pages to estimate these costs.

Startup Expenses

Type of Operation	Home Office	Rented Office Space
Rent (security deposit and first six months)	$0	$4,200
Office equipment, furniture, supplies	$1,500	$9,500
Business licenses	$100	$100
Phone (line installation charges)	$90	$115
Utility deposits	$0	$200
Employee wages (first six months)	$0	$3,000
Start-up advertising	$100	$500
Legal services	$375	$525
Insurance (annual cost)	$125	$450
Market research	$500	$1,000
Membership dues (professional associations)	$150	$150
Publications (annual subscriptions)	$225	$225
Online service	$55	$55
Miscellaneous art supplies and equipment	$500	$750
Web hosting	$25	$25
Subtotal	$3745	$20,795
Miscellaneous expenses (add roughly 10 percent of total)	$375	$2,080
Total Startup Expenses	**$4,120**	**$22,875**

Office Equipment/Supplies

Office Equipment	
Computer	$
Scanner	
Software	
Microsoft Office	
Accounting software	
Graphic arts supplies	
Laser Printer	
Surge protector	
UPS (or battery backup)	
Digital camera	
Fax machine	
Copy machine	
Phone	
Voice mail	
Answering machine	
Postage meter/scale	
Calculator	
Office Furniture	
Desk	
Chair	
File cabinet(s)	
Bookcase	
Office Supplies	
Letterhead, envelopes, business cards	
Miscellaneous supplies (pens, folders, etc.)	
Computer /copier paper	
Extra printer cartridges	

Office Equipment/Supplies, continued

Office Supplies	
Art supplies	
Back up storage	
CD-R or DVD disks	
Mouse pad	
Total	$

Communications

All businesses need the ability to communicate with clients and prospects. A freelance graphic design business, no matter what its size, needs this capability. The basics include phone, fax, internet connectivity, e-mail, and website.

Phone

All businesses need telephone service. Your freelance graphic design business is no exception. Graphic artists use the telephone to contact clients and prospects. You will need the telephone for conference calls.

Five things you need to consider when thinking about your telephone service are:

1. *Long-distance telephone service is probably necessary.* You need affordable long-distance calling, which is easy now that some services allow unlimited long-distance service for a flat rate. Another alternative is to use long-distance calling cards, which offer long-distance service for only a few cents each minute.

2. *Voice-mail service is needed to answer your telephone when you are not in your office or busy working on assignments (especially on deadline).* Your voice mailbox should be accessible from anywhere. This allows you to pick up and respond to messages while traveling.

3. *Conference calling capacity is vital.* Telephone meetings are common for graphic designers.

4. *A hard-wired telephone should be your primary model.* You do not want to be talking to a client or source and have your conversation fade out or be interrupted by radio static.

5. *Cell phones are common among freelance graphic designers.* Replacing pagers as a way for quick contact, the cell phone is an important communications tool for the busy freelance graphic designer.

Fax

There are several options for the graphic designer when it comes to a fax machine. You can use a stand-alone fax machine, a fax modem in your computer, or use a fax-through-e-mail solution. Although some industries do not use faxes, others still rely on them heavily. As a freelance graphic designer, you are likely to send sketches and preliminary artwork via fax to some clients.

> ## Smart Tip
>
> *Tip...*
>
> You can send faxes through e-mail. Services such as efax (www.efax.com) allow you to receive faxes anytime you access your e-mail. You no longer need a dedicated telephone line or a fax machine to send and receive faxes. Services like those from efax.com costs less than maintaining a fax machine and a separate telephone line.

Internet

As a freelance graphic designer, you need an internet connection and an internet presence. Because of working with large graphic computer files, dial-up service is not an option. A high-speed cable or DSL connection is not a luxury, but rather a necessity.

E-Mail

As part of your internet presence, you need to have e-mail access. Clients and prospects will expect communication via e-mail. Your e-mail address is important here. Your options include

- web-based e-mail,
- internet service provider (ISP) e-mail, or
- a private domain.

Web-based e-mail is often free. Many of the major web companies offer e-mail service and plenty of free storage. Some sources are Gmail.com, Hotmail.com, and Yahoo.com. The advantage of using web-based e-mail, in addition to being free, is that your e-mail address can remain constant. You can access your e-mail anywhere you have access to a computer with web connectivity.

You must consider what type of image your e-mail address presents. You should have a typical e-mail address, such as mt@aol.com, mthomas@hotmail.com, mary thomas@msn.com, or mary@thomasdesign.com.

Your e-mail address should be neutral and normal, not be offensive in any way. Questionable e-mail addresses that have a sexual connotation, suggest dubious activities, are just distasteful, do not present a professional image, or do your business any good. In other words, they are likely to hurt your freelance graphic design business. Some bad examples are woman hater@aol.com, thorehinny@gmail.com, the hacker @hotmail.com, and finallyavailable@yahoo.com.

> **Smart Tip** *Tip...*
> Routinely send yourself an e-mail message to check its appearance. Reply to that e-mail to make sure everything in your set up is still working properly.

Being "cool" is not the attribute you want your e-mail address to convey. You must be a professional businessperson. Be careful with your online persona, especially as it relates to your business image.

E-mail software setup is important. Make sure your e-mail software is properly installed and set up. Make certain your name is appearing correctly in the "From:" box. Make sure you have your correct e-mail address in the return section, so if prospects or clients attempt to reply, they really can send a message to you without any effort.

Website

Setting up your website should be one of your earliest activities. This is often your first marketing project. As part of the process, you should purchase your own domain name. Most likely, it will coincide with the selection of your business name, described earlier in this chapter. Your business name may be selected because of what is—or is not—available as a domain name. For example, you might want to use Thomas Design as your business name, but you find that the domain "thomasdesign.com" is not available. Accordingly, you must look for another business name.

> **Beware!**
> You might be zoned out of business.
> Local zoning regulations often prohibit businesses in specific areas. This can include home offices. What might be legal in one town could be strictly prohibited in another. Check with the zoning board of your municipality.

Ordering your domain name or checking for availability is easy. Websites such as GoDaddy (www.godaddy.com) make the process fast and simple. You can easily check to see what domains are available. For less than $10, you can reserve and order your domain name.

Licenses for Your Office

After you have decided where your office is located and the business name for your freelance graphic design business, you may—or

SCORE for You

One fast way to make sure you have complied with all local regulations and laws is to consult an experienced businessperson. You can find this kind of advice quickly by contacting SCORE.

The SCORE Association (Service Corps of Retired Executives) is dedicated to entrepreneurial education and the formation, growth, and success of small businesses nationwide. There are more than 10,000 volunteers in 374 chapters operating in over 800 locations. The contact information is:

SCORE

1175 Herndon Parkway, Suite 900

Herndon, VA 20170

Phone: (800) 634-0245 or (703) 487-3612

Fax: (703) 487-3066

www.score.org

may not—need to apply for a business license to operate. Some municipalities require businesses to have a license, while others have no such requirement. Others require a license or special permit depending on your physical location.

A quick phone call to the town hall will determine if you need a license. Most licenses, where required, are not expensive. But you cannot launch your business without one.

You may also need to apply for a sales tax license. This again varies among locations. Check with your local taxing authority.

Legal
Issues

As a graphic artist or designer, you create art and designs, in various forms and media. Most of what is created is done on assignment or commission. But who owns the design? The answers are in U.S. copyright law.

When you create a work, you automatically own the copyright to that work for your lifetime, plus 70 years.

However, many clients want to control the design. They want you to do the work, pay you for it at the agreed price, and then own what you created. If you agree, there should be no problem. However, there could be, if you do not handle the issue of copyright correctly.

It's far beyond the scope of this book to turn you into an expert in copyright law. In fact, attorneys specialize in this area of complicated law, often referred to as *intellectual property*. For specific legal questions, as always, you should consult with your lawyer. However, as a freelance graphic design businessperson, you do need to understand the basics and comply with the law, as well as work with your clients as you produce copyrightable material and designs.

Understanding Copyright

Copyright law is a legal issue that designers must consider when they work for others. The U.S. copyright laws protect your creative property. Under the law, copyright protection covers five basic categories:

1. reproduction rights;
2. derivative rights, the right to create adaptations of an original work;
3. distribution rights, the right to sell a work;
4. display rights; and
5. performance rights.

Graphic artists may find their work in any of these categories. Generally speaking, for designers and illustrators, reproduction and derivative rights are the most important areas of copyright law.

What Copyright Protects

The U.S. copyright law protects "original works of authorship" that are fixed in a tangible form of expression. The fixation need not be directly perceptible so long as it may be communicated with the aid of a machine or device. According to the U.S. copyright office, copyrightable works include

- literary works;
- musical works, including any accompanying words;
- dramatic works, including any accompanying music;
- pantomimes and choreographic works;
- pictorial, graphic, and sculptural works;

- motion pictures and other audiovisual works;
- sound recordings; and
- architectural works.

The copyright office says these categories should be viewed broadly. For example, computer programs and most "compilations" may be registered as "literary works." Maps and architectural plans may be registered as "pictorial, graphic, and sculptural works."

Understanding Visual Arts Works

According to the copyright office, visual arts works are defined as original pictorial, graphic, and sculptural works that include two-dimensional and three-dimensional works of fine, graphic, and applied art. For the purpose of copyright, examples of visual arts works include:

- Advertisements, commercial prints, labels
- Artificial flowers and plants
- Artwork applied to clothing or to other useful articles
- Bumper stickers, decals, stickers
- Cartographic works, such as maps, globes, relief models
- Cartoons, comic strips
- Collages
- Dolls, toys
- Drawings, paintings, murals
- Enamel works
- Fabric, floor, and wallcovering designs
- Games, puzzles
- Greeting cards, postcards, stationery
- Holograms, computer and laser artwork
- Jewelry designs
- Models
- Mosaics
- Needlework and craft kits
- Original prints, such as engravings, etchings, serigraphs, silk screen prints, woodblock prints
- Patterns for sewing, knitting, crochet, needlework

- Photographs, photomontages
- Posters
- Record jacket artwork or photography
- Relief and intaglio prints
- Reproductions, such as lithographs, collotypes
- Sculpture, such as carvings, ceramics, figurines, maquettes, molds, relief sculptures
- Stained glass designs
- Stencils, cut-outs
- Technical drawings, architectural drawings or plans, blueprints, diagrams, mechanical drawings
- Weaving designs, lace designs, tapestries

What Copyright Does Not Protect

The copyright law does not cover several categories of material. The following items are generally not eligible for federal copyright protection:

- Works that have not been fixed in a tangible form of expression (for example, speeches or performances that have not been written or recorded)
- Titles, names, short phrases, and slogans; familiar symbols or designs; mere variations of typographic ornamentation, lettering, or coloring; mere listings of ingredients or contents
- Ideas, procedures, methods, systems, processes, concepts, principles, discoveries, or devices, as distinguished from a description, explanation, or illustration
- Works consisting entirely of information that is common property and containing no original authorship (for example: standard calendars, height and weight charts, tape measures and rulers, and lists or tables taken from public documents or other common sources)

> **Fun Fact**
> The Nike swoosh was designed by University of Oregon student Carolyn Davidson in 1964. Ms. Davidson was paid a total of $35 for the now famous design.

The Works Made for Hire Exception

Under the law, a copyright protects a work from the time it is created in a fixed form. Only the author can rightfully claim copyright. There is, however, an exception: the copyright law defines a category of works called *works made for hire*. If a work is made for hire, the employer, and *not* the employee, is considered the author. The employer may be a firm, an organization, or an individual.

Some examples of work made for hire include:

- A newspaper reporter is employed by a newspaper publisher—what the reporter writes is owned by the paper, and not the reporter.
- A software program is created by a computer programmer employed to produce the program. The employer, and not the programmer, can claim the copyright.

Employee and Employer Relationship

Employee and employer relationships are another area of law that is involved in copyright questions. Various federal and state laws and court decisions have established definitions and tests to determine if a relationship exists.

If you are an employee, your employer is likely to claim the copyright of anything you create, whether you have signed agreement. Most employers are sophisticated enough to present their creative employees with an agreement that states this clearly. But even those that do not use a signed contract can claim the copyright.

Independent Contractor Status

Most freelance graphic designers are hired not as employees but as independent contractors. This is done to avoid tax obligations as well as other costs associated with employment, such as benefits.

When your freelance graphic design business is hired to create a copyrightable project, who owns the copyright? And if you are operating a corporation and you are its employee, doesn't your corporation own the copyright, even if you are the sole stockholder of the corporation? As you can see, these can grow into thorny situations, worthy of questions on a bar examination.

You can be sure that if your clients are paying for design work, they will also want the right to claim the work as their own, as if they had created it solely and without you and your talent. Your best option is to prevent any misunderstandings by putting your intentions in writing. If you intend to surrender all rights of your work to your client, then do so, but put it in writing. Any work made for hire (WMFH)

Tip...

Smart Tip

You can opt to submit a detailed contract to your client. However, the more legal contract looking your document is, the more likely your client will balk or send it to their legal department or lawyers for review. It is usually best to create a simple agreement. One that is easy to read and a page or less in length often works. Many graphic designers use nothing more than a simple business letter to resolve the copyright issue.

Getting Paid by Retaining Your Rights

To make sure you get paid, you may want to include verbiage that assures payment if your client wants to control the copyright. Sample language might be, "Until full payment has been made, the designer retains full and complete ownership of all original Work Product or parts contained therein, whether preliminary or final. Upon full payment by the client, the client shall only then obtain ownership of the final Work Product to use and distribute as they see fit."

agreement must be in writing to be deemed valid. Verbal WMFH agreements are invalid and not enforceable in court.

Most often, your client will have a document ready, seeking all rights under a work made for hire agreement. Other times, you, as the freelance graphic designer, will need to provide the agreement to the client.

Length of Copyright Protection

Recent changes in the copyright laws affect works created on or after January 1, 1978. Work created on or after this date is automatically protected from the moment of its creation and is ordinarily given a term enduring for the author's life plus an additional 70 years after the author's death. For works made for hire and for anonymous and pseudonymous works (unless the author's identity is revealed in Copyright Office records), the duration of copyright will be 95 years from publication or 120 years from creation, whichever is shorter.

Smart Tip

Tip...

Even though you are transferring your right to any copyright of your work, you might want to keep one of your rights. You may want to retain the right to use the work for self-promotion. This can be done easily by adding the following to your work made for hire agreements: "The designer retains the right to use the completed Work Product and any preliminary designs for the purpose of design competitions, future publications on design, educational purposes, marketing materials, and portfolio."

Other Copyright Issues

There is much more to learn about copyright law. You should know that before you can proceed in court, you need to register your work. It's important for you to do

Work Made for Hire Agreement

The common language of a standard WMFH agreement is:

THE AUTHOR AND THE CLIENT AGREE THAT:

Title and Copyright Assignment

(a) Author and Client intend this to be a contract for services and each considers the products and results of the services to be rendered by Author hereunder (the "Work") to be a work made for hire. Author acknowledges and agrees that the Work (and all rights therein, including, without limitation, copyright) belongs to and shall be the sole and exclusive property of the Client.

(b) If for any reason the Work would not be considered a work made for hire under applicable law, Author does hereby sell, assign, and transfer to the Client, its successors and assigns, the entire right, title and interest in and to the copyright in the Work and any registrations and copyright applications relating thereto and any renewals and extensions thereof, and in and to all works based upon, derived from, or incorporating the Work, and in an to all income, royalties, damages, claims and payments now or hereafter due or payable with respect thereto, and in and to all causes of action, either in law or in equity for past, present, or future infringement based on the copyrights, and in and to all rights corresponding to the foregoing throughout the world.

(c) If the Work is one to which the provisions of 17 U.S.C. 106A apply, the Author hereby waives and appoints the Client to assert on the Author's behalf the Author's moral rights or any equivalent rights regarding the form or extent of any alteration to the Work (including, without limitation, removal or destruction) or the making of any derivative works based on the Work, including, without limitation, photographs, drawings or other visual reproductions or the Work, in any medium, for the client's purposes.

(d) Author agrees to execute all papers and to perform such other proper acts as the Client may deem necessary to secure for Client or its designee the rights herein assigned.

▲

Bright Idea

Since you cannot use the courts to protect your work unless it is registered in the Library of Congress, it's a good idea to register all the work you make public.

this in a timely manner. If you register your work within three months of making it public, you will be entitled to recover attorney's fees and statutory damages. If you file your registration after the initial three-month period, you will only be entitled to those damages that you can actually prove.

Copyright law is always changing. Court decisions and amendments from Congress keep the laws evolving. Attorneys who specialize in intellectual property (IP) remain current on these changes. Often IP attorneys make speeches at local business meetings to explain a portion of copyright law. (It's a way they market their services and law firms.) It is to your advantage to keep current with copyright law. Try to locate local IP attorneys in your area, and attend any public function where you can hear them speak on the topic.

Copyright Registration

Filing a copyright registration is not difficult. You can file the registration yourself without the assistance of an attorney. Artwork is registered on copyright Form VA, available from the U.S. copyright office by calling the copyright forms number at (202) 707-9100 or by visiting www.copyright.gov. Cost is $45 (payable by check) to register each work.

Always remember to keep copies of everything you use to file your copyright registration. Be patient, as it often takes three to four months to receive your copyright registration with your registration number.

Tip...

Smart Tip

You can group together your artwork into a collection to avoid registering each item separately.

Notice of Copyright

Always place a copyright notice on your work. Every design, every disk, and every digital file needs your copyright notice, if you want to protect your work.

The form of the copyright notice is:

© Your Name Here 2009

Copyright Your Name Here 2009

Copr. Your Name Here 2009

Protecting Your Copyrighted Images

Graphic designers can have difficulty protecting their work in a digital world. Online images are so easy to click and save and can be used without your permission by the uneducated or the dishonest. Some people wrongly believe everything on the internet is free and public property. Consider these three steps to help protect your work:

1. Be sure to put your copyright notice (© Your Name Here 2009) on every photo, illustration, or web page you post online.
2. Make images and graphics harder to "borrow." Reduce the image size for screen viewing. Lower the image resolution to 72 dpi and size it to 300 pixels or smaller on the longest side. Sizing the images smaller makes them less suitable to print, but it still provides an adequate screen image for viewing.
3. Use electronic watermarking to protect your images.

Contacting the Copyright Office

The U.S. copyright office provides circulars, announcements, regulations, other related materials, and all copyright application forms. The fastest way to obtain these materials is via the internet. The copyright office homepage is www.copyright.gov.

You may also write to the copyright office at:

> Library of Congress
> Copyright Office
> Public Information Office
> 101 Independence Avenue, SE
> Washington, DC 20559-6000

Information is available by telephone: For information about copyright, call the Public Information Office at (202) 707-3000. Information specialists are on duty from 8:30 A.M. to 5 P.M. eastern time, Monday through Friday, except on federal holidays. Recorded information is available 24 hours a day.

If you know which application forms and circulars you want, request them 24 hours a day from the Forms and Publications Hotline at (202) 707-9100. Leave a recorded message on the voice mail.

When Not to Protect Your Copyright

Some things you create you may want to protect with a copyright. There are other cases in which as a freelance graphic designer you will need to assign the copyright to your client. A good example is a logo. If you created a logo for a client, you can be sure that the client will want to use that logo on everything, from business cards to coffee cups. That's why the client came to you in the first place: to create a logo that can be used in many ways.

To attempt to claim copyright on a client's logo is likely to make you look silly or immature as a businessperson. Don't try to control a client's product with the copyright laws. Realize up front why the client is seeking your services, and adjust your use of the copyright accordingly.

Seeking Competent Legal Advice

As you can see, there is a great deal of information about copyright law. There are volumes of published material on the subject, and it is evolving and changing.

Don't overlook the importance of seeking competent legal advice as you move forward with your freelance graphic design business. Your attorney can explain your duties, obligations, and rights to you. Remember, too, that it is always cheaper to keep yourself out of trouble than it is to extract yourself from a legal problem. Always seek competent counsel for any legal issue.

Launching Your Freelance Graphic Design Business

By this point, your graphic design business is taking shape. A business plan has been carefully prepared. You know the name of your enterprise, its legal business structure, and its location. Your office and work areas are set up.

You are ready for business, but you need to be in business. It's time to launch, to announce to the world that you are ready and available for work. You have several different options on how you launch your business. Some designers choose a low-key approach while others use a loud, flashy event to announce the opening of their design business. It's up to you, but it should be a planned, not a haphazard event.

So You're a Graphic Designer?

Well, you know you are a graphic designer, but who else knows of your artistry? And most importantly, who knows that you are looking for graphic design assignments? As you launch your freelance graphic design business, it's time to announce to the world that your doors are open and you're looking for business. You should approach this with a well-thought out plan. By doing so, you can get maximum impact from this milestone event.

Your First Client

Your first client for your new graphic design business should be you!

Before launching to the world, you should create a design for your business. It should include:

- Logo
- Business cards
- Stationery
- Brochure(s)
- Signage (if a sign is to be used at your studio/office)
- Website

Your design for your own business will be one of the first things potential clients use to judge your work. As a graphic designer, you should have no trouble producing your own creative image.

Of course, all must be completed before you launch your grand opening. You never want to tell clients that you are too busy to do their work. And if you don't have the time to get your own work completed, you are not likely to get their work done either.

Your Portfolio

Get yourself prepared for your launch by perfecting your portfolio. You need to make sure that only your best work is there, and ready to be shown to potential clients. Assemble the best, and get ready to launch!

Getting the Word Out

Publicity is the most cost-effective method to launch your new graphic design business. It works best, regardless of whether your market is local, regional, or national. With an effective publicity plan, you can reach hundreds or thousands of potential clients virtually overnight. You are introduced by media, which gives you instant credibility. What might normally be a sales pitch is often repackaged into a news story. This grants you trustworthiness and standing with potential clients.

The launch of your new graphic design business is newsworthy. Don't overlook it as an event that can generate positive publicity and notice for you in your marketplace. If you aren't sure how to get attention, read up on public relations (PR). There are numerous books about business publicity. You can learn the basics from them.

Bright Idea

Seeking press coverage is much like playing the lottery. You can win a little, or a lot. By seeking press coverage, you can gain publicity. You are considered newsworthy and above the rest when you are featured in news articles or television news stories. This exposure often makes your phone ring with potential clients. To get the coverage, just like a lottery, you have to play to win.

Getting the Business Community's Attention

Your market needs to know about your new freelance graphic design business. A press release that is well thought out and crafted can help increase your visibility almost overnight. Because the majority of your business will be from other businesses, you need to focus on getting their attention. By this point, you certainly know your target market. It might be new businesses or businesses in a specific industry (hospitality, financial, manufacturing). Whatever your target, you proceed accordingly.

Smart Tip

Don't forget to leverage every bit of press coverage you receive. Keep copies of every article and every mention in the press. Put all your coverage on your website. Add it to your marketing kit, and send pieces to clients, prospects, colleagues, and professional organizations.

Press Release

Carefully craft your press release. Make variations that appeal to different segments of the marketplace or news outlets. Time the submission of your press release with your entire new business launch. Obviously, you do not

Bright Idea

Radiate the aura of already having achieved fame as a graphic designer. Psychological studies reveal that when individuals carry themselves with the impression of someone who has achieved recognition, others perceive them as actually having it. This is what publicity and public relations is all about. Toot your own horn, especially if you have a good sounding one.

want press coverage and publicity if your new telephone number is not working or your website is in the process of being completed.

Send your releases directly to an editor at the local paper. And don't overlook other local outlets, including radio stations, those small throw-away newspapers, weekly newspapers, television stations, and business journals or magazines. Be sure to release your press release on free resources, such as PRweb.com. Your press releases should also be posted on your website.

News reporters and journalists are always looking for "fresh meat." They want your story, especially if it is interesting. The more you can give them other than "just another business opening," the more likely you will receive good coverage. What makes you or your graphic design business unique? (Look in your business plan for this answer.) Will you be working with specialized industries or businesses?

Don't be afraid to feed reporters (or others) fresh meat by finding a great hook. For example, if you are a retired police officer, feed them a headline like "Ex-Cop Opens Design Studio." The more creative and interesting you are, the more coverage you'll receive from the media.

Why Use Press Releases

The most compelling reason to use a press release is that it is the standard method of communicating your news to your intended target, editors and reporters in newsrooms. Because of its format, combining a headline with a simple to-the-point message and an opening paragraph describing what the news actually is, it is easy for the assignment editor to quickly scan your release to see if it's relevant. If so, she will read the body of the release for additional information—and your contact information.

Press releases have been the standard method of disseminating news for decades, and every editor, reporter, and journalist has learned to both loathe and rely on them. Some major outlets like the *New York Times* receive up to 5,000 press releases a week, and they diligently peruse each one when properly submitted. See the Sample Press Release on page 63.

Smart Tip

Tip...

Company launches are always considered newsworthy events. Make sure you get your coverage by submitting a well-crafted press release.

Sample Press Release

Whitney & Bailey, LLC, a full service graphic design business, is pleased to announce the opening of its design studio in Canton. Jonathan Whitney, one of the founding partners, says the new firm will focus on providing design services for institutional, government, and private/public sector clients.

Mr. Whitney has over 22 years of industry experience, most recently as a supervising graphic design for the Cochran Design Group. In this role, he directed many complex and notable projects, including the Convention Center media makeover design.

The new design firm will employ three designers initially, with more staff to be added early next year. The firm is establishing its offices in the downtown revitalization district, in the Oblender Office Suite. It is opening Monday, April 20.

Be sure to include contact information, including phone numbers, e-mail addresses, and website. Make it easy—and not difficult—for reporters and editors to contact you for more information, to ask questions, and to interview you.

In today's busy information world, a press release is what an editor expects to see. You must use one if you want to get the word out to the media about your news or product launch. Your press release should be well-written and concise. Keep the length of your announcement to two pages—or less. Editors and journalists have a limited attention span and want to know as much as possible in a short amount of time. Your best response will be from shorter—not longer—press releases. Keep the body of your press release simple as in the sample above.

Announcement Letters

Most new businesses send announcement letters to potential clients. It's common to send a letter to potential clients, similar to the sample on page 64.

The letter can be modified to include statements such as "specializing in the hospitality industry." As a graphic designer, you can target those industries or businesses where you have specialized knowledge or skills.

Sample Announcement Letter

Dear _____:

I am pleased to announce that beginning April 20, I am offering graphic design services. As a graphic artist and designer for the past 12 years, I have produced:

- Business logos

- Websites

- Brochures, business documents, and product packaging

- Billboards, corporate reports, and display advertising

I believe in graphic design that conveys strong visual messages and enhances product, service, and company branding.

If you need help with your company's image or a new design project, call me now. Design fees are affordable and arranged on an individual basis.

Sincerely,

Mary Thomas

Graphic Designer

Contact Your Competition

As part of your announcement phase of the launch of your freelance graphic design business, be sure to contact your competition. Let them know you are available for assignments, especially for any overflow work they might have. At the same time, make sure you request information from them, so you can refer or subcontract work to them should you become too busy to handle all your work assignments.

Size of Opening

As you plan the launch of your freelance graphic design business, remember that your launch can be on a large or small scale. It is really up to you, your style, and your location. Obviously, it is difficult to have a huge open house event if your graphic design studio is located in a spare bedroom in your apartment. If you have rented commercial space, it is easier to hold a glitzier affair.

No matter what the size or nature of your business, be sure to coordinate the announcement and launch of your new venture. Doing so forces you to meet an important deadline and milestone.

And don't forget to have fun. Much of the world of work has to be serious, but opening your own graphic design company, and its actual launch, should be one of the fun times you have in business. No matter what the size of the event, enjoy the moment you finally open.

Finding Your First Customers

Success in any business results from finding customers. Providing excellent service and reasonable prices is what builds an enterprise. Finding your first customers should come about from your successful business launch. It is the beginning of the marketing effort.

In Chapter 7, your marketing plan will be discussed in detail. The launching of your graphic design business is the first step in getting your business going. You want to be able to sustain it and grow it.

In the beginning, it is a great balancing act. You must keep your initial customers happy by providing great service, and you must keep searching for new clients. Don't overlook either responsibility.

7

Marketing
Yourself

Part of the mystery of —and the answer to— operating a successful freelance graphic design business is marketing. It's a never-ending process, and one of the major differences between working for someone else as a graphic designer and operating your own graphic design business. Marketing involves keeping your name out there in the marketplace, letting people know you are ready and available for work. You cannot stop marketing, even if you are busy and have plenty of work at the moment.

The world has an abundance of good graphic artists who will never profit from their talents because although they are really good at what they do, they are not good at marketing. Much of your freelance business success or failure is related directly to the marketing of your service. Always keep in mind that it's not what you do that determines your success, but how you market what you do.

Developing Your Marketing Plan

If you're a self-starter, you have probably already thought about marketing your graphic design business. That is one of the earliest things you need to consider when you think about starting out on your own because your marketing plan is critically important to the success of your business. Your plan, once launched, will determine your income and profitability.

Some people starting a business approach the marketing aspect in a slovenly manner. That's a huge mistake. Marketing is a lot more than simply placing an advertisement and hoping people will call and buy your service.

Your marketing plan should be precise and in writing. It should include those steps you will take, and the order you will take them in, to market your business. As you develop your marketing plan, list those activities that you will do as part of your effort to promote your self.

Marketing need not be expensive. You do not need to spend thousands of dollars on advertising. In fact, you might find that your best marketing strategies will cost little and take little effort to launch.

There are a variety of things you could do, including launching expensive advertising and marketing campaigns. You could, for example, sponsor expensive golf outings with open bars and food buffets. But this approach would put a huge dent in your bank account very quickly.

> **Tip...**
>
> **Smart Tip**
> You can do low cost marketing. For example, you could teach a course on graphic design at your local community college, or present a seminar at a local chamber of commerce meeting on how to design a newsletter. Both of these activities would market your name and service and instead of costing you money, could actually produce some income.

Don't take on marketing that you don't enjoy. If you do not like to speak in public, then don't seek to market by speaking at service group meetings. But if you do possess the gift of gab and like talking to groups, find a topic about graphic design and offer to speak. Speaking is a form of marketing that costs you next to nothing to implement, yet can result in paying jobs.

Pressing the Flesh

Get yourself out to those who are likely to need your services and hire you. The more people you can meet, the better your chances of developing a client base.

"First, commit to a market," advises Ilise Benun, the author of *Stop Pushing Me Around: A Workplace Guide for the Timid, Shy and Less Assertive* and *Designing Websites for Every Audience*. "Contrary to what you may want to believe, the whole world is not your market. Even if everybody CAN use your services, you can't market to everyone; it's physically impossible, and trying to do so will only waste your marketing efforts."

Benun says that graphic designers should follow some simple advice when it comes to targeting prospects and marketing their graphic design business. "Don't let the fact that everybody could be a prospect get in the way of making the decisions to target a specific and identifiable market. In reality, there are only a few specific groups with a need or desire for the special benefits you offer. Your job is to find those "niche" markets and commit your efforts to getting business from them, one at a time. It will not limit you; indeed, it will free you."

The founder of Marketing Mentor, a one-on-one coaching program for designers and other creatives, Benun offers e-mail tips from her website at: www.marketing-mentor tips.com and on

> ## Bright Idea
> "The best list for you is the list of people with whom you have already begun the process of building a relationship," says Ilise Benun. "Don't underestimate its value for a minute. These people already know you, and may even trust you (at least more than those on the mailing list you're thinking of renting), which means that the amount of time it will take to make the sale is shorter."

her blog, www.marketingmixblog.com. She often advises graphic designers how to build a marketing list. "To build on that list, choose marketing tools that motivate qualified prospects to raise their hands and ask you to market to them—tools like publicity and press coverage, offers of free samples, and email newsletters," she tells her clients.

There are many resources for acquiring a list of prospects, especially if you don't need thousands of them, and you probably don't. The most effective list is generally one you create yourself, based on the criteria you've chosen (size of company, revenue, number of employees, etc.). Although it requires a bit more work on your part, compiling and collecting names for your own list makes for a much more effective and profitable list.

"Be wary of someone selling prospect lists," Benun advises, "because although they sound good and are often very inexpensive, the people on the list may be someone's prospects, but they are not usually yours."

You probably have access to lists that you may not be aware of, so look first to your own resources. Here are some of the places Benun directs her clients to look for prospects:

- *Industry and trade group directories.* Almost every trade group publishes a directory, either online and/or printed. As a member of a group, one of the benefits you get is access to (and inclusion in) the member directory. (Some groups even make their directory available for a fee, so you don't even have to join.) You may not realize it, but this valuable resource is one of the best reasons to join a group. Directories are invaluable because they prequalify your prospects and give you the names of people to start with, which saves your valuable time. Calling a company and trying to find the person who hires or buys the services you're offering is very time consuming.

- *Attendee lists to industry events.* Often, a list of attendees is published and distributed to attendees of an industry event or conference—it's one of the perks of attending. This is another invaluable resource that you should do more than just glance at to see who's in attendance.

- *Resource lists published in trade publications.* Many trade publications offer (usually around year-end) annual lists of the top players in a particular industry, complete with contact information and details about the products and services offered by the company. This is not only a great source of prospects but will also give a good overview of an industry that you may be considering getting into. Keep your eyes open for these lists and use them 'til they're dog-eared.

"Also, reach out to people you read about in a trade journal or local online news source," Benun says. "Always keep your eyes open for the choice prospects here and there whose names you come across in a magazine article. Write them a letter, send them an e-mail message, or just pick up the phone and call to introduce yourself. This is a cold call, yes, but what makes this kind of cold call instantly warm is the feeling behind your response, your genuine interest in this company. It's very flattering to your prospect (providing it's true, of course) to hear that you are calling because you have chosen them based on what you know, what you've seen, and what you have to offer. If there really is a fit that you can describe clearly, they just might agree to meet you. And that may well develop into a lucrative and productive working relationship, either now or later (but only if you follow up)."

Designing Your Networking

Maintaining your network of industry contacts can bring in new business to your graphic design business. This is an inexpensive yet effective method of marketing your design business.

"Word-of-mouth is always the best. Keep good relationships with client contacts, even if you stop doing work with them," advises Kensington, Maryland-based graphic designer Brent Almond. "I've gotten three new clients recently from contacts that switched jobs and called me for work at their new company."

Another graphic designer who uses a network to market is Petrula Vrontikis. "Most of our business finds us because of great word-of-mouth and referrals from our existing clients," she says. "Recently I tracked where my business has come from over the years—I created a client "family tree." More than 75 percent of my work over the last 18 years has come from my ongoing relationship with one smart, well-connected marketing director. She takes us with her when she makes career moves, and we often retain work from the organizations she's moved on from. She's referred us to her business colleagues in various industries."

Vrontikis, based in Los Angeles, is the creative director of Vrontikis Design Office. With over 23 years of experience, she adds, "The bottom line is that doing good work for smart, well-connected clients is the best business development strategy for a small design office. We work very hard to stay deserving of the comment: 'They are a pleasure to work with.'"

"Meeting your prospects in person is, hands down, one of the best ways to make a strong impression, find out what they need, and get their contact information," adds Ilise Benun, the Hoboken, New Jersey-based consultant. "And yet, so many designers don't want to leave their studios, much less find the places where their prospects gather."

Benun said there are tons of networking events to attend, too many actually, too many ways to meet people you'll never see again, too many opportunities to collect a stack of business cards you'll never look at again. But networking is not a contest, and it's not about schmoozing."

She offered this list of do's and don'ts when networking:

- *Find low-key learning environments.* Business card exchanges and other networking events are high-pressure situations where people go to meet others but usually do so with all their defenses intact. For more relaxed networking, find educational atmospheres, such as workshops and seminars, where the focus is on learning and people's defenses are lower.

- *Start conversations.* Go out of your way to get into conversations with anyone and everyone you can, in person, on the phone, or via e-mail. Cross the street, cross the room, cross the train to talk to people. Find out what they're working on, and tell them what you're working on. Anything can come out of a simple conversation: ideas, alliances, connections, referrals, new business, new opportunities.

- *Make contact, not contacts.* The goal of networking is not to meet as many people as possible in as short a time as possible. The goal is to find a business community that satisfies your needs, one that brings together people who are your prospects and with whom you are comfortable. So if you attend an event, don't think you have to get to everyone in the room. Meet as many people as you can but also, if a conversation is going well, stay with it.

- *Be a good listener.* Don't be worried about what you're going to say. You don't need to perform your sales pitch, just have your blurbs ready to use as a tool to engage people in conversation. Do more listening than talking, and ask a lot of questions. Then simply respond to what you hear. Answer questions, devise solutions, be creative. Sounds easy? Just try it.

- *Arrive early.* If you wait until most of the attendees are already there, many of them will already be in conversations and it won't be as easy to break in.

- *Never sit with someone you know.* Attend an event with a friend, but put on your nametags and then separate at the door. Otherwise, you will never meet anyone new.

- *Look for wallflowers.* Instead of trying to break into conversations that are already going, find someone sitting or standing alone and simply introduce yourself. Do it even if they don't look like they want to be approached. The apparent standoffishness may merely be a cover for their own discomfort.

- *Use the food to begin conversations.* Stand by the buffet and make recommendations to anyone who approaches about what's good (or bad).

- *Keep going back to the buffet.* Never put more than three bites on your plate. Take your plate to a crowded table, introduce yourself, talk (and listen) for 10 to 15 minutes, exchange cards, then excuse yourself to get up and get more food. (After all, your plate will be empty.) Repeat this until the room is empty. And don't forget that you can also talk to people in line at the buffet.

- *Be random about where you sit.* You can't tell by how someone looks what will come out of a conversation with them. Don't judge.

- *Make notes about the people you meet.* Every time someone gives you a card, make a point of writing a note on the back—while you're still talking. This will not only flatter, but you will have a much better chance of remembering what you talked about so that you can follow up in a more personal way.

- *Wear a jacket with pockets.* Keep your business cards and a pen in the left pocket and put any cards you get into the right pocket. That way you won't be fumbling with cards or accidentally hand a new contact someone else's card.

- *Wear an unusual accessory*. Choose a colorful scarf or tie so that when you follow up you can also remind them who you are by referring to that accessory, as in, "I was the one with the orange scarf."

Half the Work Is Finding the Work

In the beginning, half of your work as a graphic designer is finding the work. The good news is that current graphic designers reduce the amount of time they spend hunting for work after their business is established. Demand is then so high that they can keep busy from referrals and repeat work from clients. However, in the beginning, you must spend time looking for good clients and customers, and interesting work projects.

Seeking Referrals

Referrals are an easy way to introduce yourself and your service to people you don't already know.

Ask people you know for leads and referrals of people they know who might use your services. That's what Petrula Vrontikis did to expand her graphic design business. "There have been times when I have contacted my vendors and ongoing clients, asking for leads," she says. "This has been somewhat successful, as I am at an advantage contacting them based on the introduction of someone they already know and trust."

Bright Idea
Seeking referrals should be a part of a graphic artist's marketing plan. It's a fast way to develop business and a very low-cost method of marketing your business.

"My business has come mostly from referrals or repeat business," says Mary Cronin, the Ann Arbor, Michigan, graphic designer. "I joined a local business networking organization a few years ago and that relationship has brought me several new clients and more exposure."

Experienced and established graphic designers rely heavily on referrals to keep work in their queue. Keeping in touch with those you've met in the past makes sense. Sending holiday greeting cards is one way experienced designers maintain contact.

Cold Calling Does Work

Many people think that cold calling does not work. That's because consumer's don't like unsolicited phone calls. For business to business marketing, cold calling does work. The first thing you need to consider when cold calling is that you're not there to outsmart your potential customers, but to inform them about your graphic design business.

Develop a good pitch that alerts your prospect that you are not there to sell to everyone. The idea of selling to a limited customer base can be appealing to some. The idea of exclusivity has benefits. As a graphic designer, you can only work for a limited number of clients. You can often use this limitation as part of your pitch to potential clients.

It might be difficult to start cold calling because of its perception, but overcoming it is just as easy as picking up the phone. As you refine your pitch and perfect your offer, you can turn prospects into customer by selling your design services.

Here are five cold-calling tips from Ilise Benun

1. *Tell them right away where you found them.* People become instantly more receptive when you begin by saying, "I got your name from . . ." Whether it's from a list, a colleague or the media, reveal your sources.

2. *Ask if it's a good time to talk.* Before you launch into your intro, be sure they're available. Your sensitivity and respect will be appreciated.

3. *Don't rush to speak with your prospect.* Get as much information from the screener as possible so that when you speak to the "buyer," they see you took the time to do your research.

4. *Get them talking and listen to the answers.* You don't have to do all the talking— in fact, you shouldn't. Ask the questions that uncover needs you can address directly, rather than wasting everyone's time on what you assume they need.

5. *Use a script or outline.* It helps to have a script, but you don't have to be locked into it. The purpose of a script is to guide you, to get you started, to provide structure. It can be especially helpful when your prospect doesn't respond as you expect, potentially causing you to forget your most important question.

Marketing consultant Ilise Benun was asked if she recommended a graphic designer call prospects first or send something first and then call. "A debate rages on this question, and there's no right answer, Benun says. "However,

. . . if you don't have the name of the person who buys creative services, always make a research call first to get that information. You'll never be able to follow up on a letter sent via snail mail to a title, like "Corporate Marketing Director."

. . . if you do have a contact name but no connection to the person, you should also call first to make sure that person is a qualified prospect for your services. If they're not and you send them an expensive package (or even a simple letter), you've wasted much more time than you would have spent making the initial research call."

The only time to send something first is:

1. when you have the name of someone you are sure buys design services, AND
2. you have a marketing piece that will really stand out from the clutter.

Internet Marketing

Today's freelance graphic designers rely on the internet to market their services. A website is not a luxury, but rather a necessity. It is the first thing you need to launch as part of your marketing campaign.

"My website is the first place referrals go to learn more about my services and see examples of past projects," graphic designer Mary Cronin says. When asked how he markets his graphic design business, Brent Almond said, "Mainly through my website."

Today's websites are used as portfolios. No matter how you initially contact prospects or potential clients, you can expect them to look at your website for samples of your work.

Blogging for Graphic Designers

Should a graphic designer have a blog? "That's the *question du jour* these days," says graphic designer marketing consultant Benun. And her answer is, "It depends." "If you already have a website and are trying to decide between an e-mail newsletter and a blog, note the main difference: a blog is a "pull" (i.e., readers have to find it and go there) while an e-mail marketing message or newsletter is a "push" (i.e., you send or push it to those you want to keep in touch with)," Benun says. "Actually, these two tools can work beautifully together. You can drive traffic to your blog by including links to it in your e-mail messages."

She said that blogs are less promotional and less formal than a traditional static website, so you can speak in your "everyday" voice, which is often more friendly and approachable. Also, you can combine personal and professional elements in your blog: how much depends on what you're comfortable with, and what your prospective clientele will be comfortable reading about you.

"Also, blogging is improved by visuals, so designers are perfectly positioned to show their style. A small description, a bit of info or counterpoint to the image, and you're done," Benun says.

But is a blog an effective marketing tool? "It can be, but it's indirect. You shouldn't expect to "get work" from your blog, although it does happen. More than a traditional website, a blog has the potential to convey your design sensibility and who you are as a person, and that's often what will help you stand out from the crowd."

Who Needs You Now?

There are a variety of websites, from CraigsList to elance, where people who need graphic designers for freelance jobs post their projects. Many of these projects are small, one-time opportunities.

Ads are always a source of potential business. People seeking persons to help with projects are easy to find and contact. It only takes a minimum amount of time to look for these jobs. Those that you are contacting—by phone, e-mail, or fax—are looking for a graphic designer and receptive to your inquiry.

> **Beware!**
> Project websites often require you to get into a bidding war. Some of the those you might be bidding against are not true graphic artists or designers, but rather people who have purchased software and are simply looking for work. Don't allow yourself to get caught up in a bidding frenzy that spirals downward.

Always Marketing

Remember that you must always keep on marketing your graphic design business. Staying visible is important. Keeping in contact with past customers, as well as seeking new prospects, is essential for your business to grow, as well as remain vital. Experienced freelance graphic designers spend time on their own websites. "I've also gotten a couple of good clients who found me on industry websites," says Brent Almond.

Sending items that showcase your work also makes sense. From post cards to calendars, you should consider direct mailing campaigns. Maintaining a mailing list of prospects and past clients is a good investment of time and money. Keeping your work in front of people you are trying to influence is essential.

"And my holiday cards/client gifts always get lots of compliments, and remind existing clients to give me a call," Brent Almond says.

Rules You
Cannot Break

As a freelance graphic designer operating your own business, there are many things to concern you. Government regulations, ordinances, and laws are just some of the topics that require your attention. And if that is not enough, there are still other areas that require your attention—and all of this is beyond the actual creation of designs and art for your clients.

All of these issues fall under the category of rules that you cannot break. To be successful as a freelance graphic designer, you must do more than create and deliver great product and service. You must also follow the rules of the graphic design business. Many are common sense, while others are not as apparent.

Dealing with Clients

All of your clients will expect you to adhere to the highest ethical standards. Some clients will have established a comprehensive corporate integrity program to ensure that its vendors, consultants, officers, and employees at all levels perform their duties consistent with the requirements of public law and the policies of the corporation. Others will have a less formal approach to ethics, but still you must, as a freelance graphic designer, always provide fair, open, and ethical service to all clients.

One of your first legal obligations is to provide pricing to all customers. You cannot, for example, charge one customer a different price per hour than another, when you are doing the same kind of work. The easiest way to solve this problem is to establish a written price list.

Some graphic designers work on an hourly rate, while others work on a project basis. Project pricing is often derived from an estimate of the number of hours it will take to complete the work, multiplied by an hourly rate. Fair business laws and doctrine demand that your pricing as a graphic designer be uniform to all clients and customers.

Ethics

Your clients and customers will expect an open and honest business relationship with you, based on quality, service, and price. This expectation can only be achieved when there is a fair, open, and honest relationship between you and your clients, and both adhere to ethical business practices.

Sometimes, your clients may suggest that you do something unethical, or even illegal. Most of the time, this is done out of ignorance of laws or an ethical standard. For example, your client might ask you to use copyrighted material (photographs, text, etc.) as part of a website. You cannot do this either legally or ethically.

Beware!
Clients might ask you to give them illegal copies of copyright protected software. Don't do it! Not only is this wrong, it is illegal. You could face either criminal or civil penalties, including fines or imprisonment. Most clients that ask such things are ignorant of the laws. Your best approach is to educate them, and inform them that you would not do anything unethical or hurtful to their business or organization.

Your ethics must include the giving of business gifts. Many businesses and organizations will permit employees to accept a gift, but only those items that have a maximum value of $25 to $50. A gift with a higher valued could be (and usually is) reasonably inferred to be intended to influence the employee in the performance of their official duties.

Smart Tip

Don't put a client's employee in an uncomfortable position by presenting a gift in excess of the amount they are permitted to accept.

Another area of ethics that a freelance graphic designer must consider is conflict of interest. You cannot place yourself in a position where you are working with two competitors. This could easily happen, often innocently. Suppose one of your clients is a large, local car dealership. A direct competitor of that dealership approaches you and asks you to work for them, too.

Your work could involve working on advertising campaigns and marketing plans. Knowing what the one competitor is doing because of your inside knowledge could set up a conflict of interest.

Obviously, you must avoid any conflict of interest situation, or even the appearance of impropriety. The easiest way to avoid problems is to turn down work or clients that have the potential to be a conflict of interest.

Sometimes, there is no conflict of interest, but the person to decide that is not you, but rather your client. For example, consider the case of the car dealership. Before taking on the second dealership (the competitor to your current client) as a client, ask your first client if it is a conflict of interest. Your first client may agree that it is fine for you to do the work for the other dealership. Or he may prefer that you don't. Follow his decision.

Bright Idea

The fact that you would check with your current client to determine if a conflict of interest exists will enhance your position with that client. Being a fair businessperson is best for long-term growth and income.

You must also beware of employing relatives of clients, or hiring people that worked for or with your competitors or other graphic designers. People who you use as vendors, employees, or subcontractors could create a conflict of interest.

Of course, there are many relationships that do not create a conflict of interest. You and your competitor might use the same graphic arts supply store. That doesn't create a conflict. However, if that supplier started telling you the inside information about your competitor, then a conflict exists. In this case, the conflict of interest hurts your competitor. But keep in mind that if a vendor would do this to your competitor, it would also do it you, too.

Professional Conduct

As a graphic designer, you must always conduct yourself professionally. Often the starting point is your morals and values. Many professional organizations of graphic designers have developed, endorsed, or created a code of ethics. The code is used by the members of the organizations as a way of endorsing fair and ethical business practices.

Some of the typical areas covered in a graphic designer's code of ethics include:

- Acquainting yourself with each client's business, and providing both honest and impartial advice
- Avoiding any type of potential conflict of interest
- Being honest and truthful in describing your education, experience, professional experience, proficiencies, and competencies
- Eliminating and refusing any form of hidden compensation or kickback
- Maintaining a commitment to the development of innovative work of the highest quality
- Maintaining the confidentiality of all client information, and not providing any inside information to any person or organization
- Providing proper acknowledgment of authorship and assistance when others have collaborated with you in creating any design
- Rejecting all forms of plagiarism or illegal copying
- Showing value and respect toward other graphic designers in fair and open competition

> **Beware!**
> Is it ever OK to use someone else's design? What about a design layout? Is it okay to lift or copy a photograph you found on the internet and use a portion of it? As you can see, these areas can cause all types of questions and issues. Don't do anything that could damage your reputation as a graphic designer.

Insurance

One of the other areas that requires the attention of the freelance graphic designer is insurance. In its simplest definition, insurance is the transfer of risk. By purchasing insurance, you are transferring the risk of losses to the insurer away from yourself. You must properly insure yourself and your graphic design business. This is easy to understand when you consider fire insurance.

Suppose you purchase $100,000 worth of fire insurance on your building. If the building is totally destroyed by fire, the insurer (an insurance company) pays you

$100,000 for your loss. You have transferred the risk of the loss caused by a fire from yourself to the insurer. This type of transfer is why you purchase insurance.

For some losses, you are often self-insured or uninsured. For example, no one insures small losses. You would not likely insure the loss of a $35 box of office supplies. Even though those supplies could be stolen or destroyed, small losses are not insured. The concept remains the same: there is no reason to transfer the risk of a small loss.

But large losses—ones you could not afford—need to be insured. It's easy to transfer the risk of loss: you simply purchase insurance.

So one of the experts you need on your side is an insurance professional. You probably need to consider purchasing several different types of insurance.

Your business property (furniture, computers, software, supplies) needs to be insured for losses. This coverage is often readily available and covers comprehensive losses from multiple perils. This means that you are covered against losses from fire, theft, windstorm, auto damage, and other similar losses.

Most property damage coverage includes a deductible. The purpose of a deductable is for you to handle your own small losses. Always consider higher deductibles to reduce insurance costs. Just make sure you can afford the loss amount of your deductible. For example, if you could only afford a $1,000 loss, don't purchase a policy with a $2,500 deductible. However, if you could afford the higher deductible, you should receive a substantially lower price on your insurance coverage. Keep in mind the principle of insurance: the transfer of risk. Transfer only the amount of risk that you cannot afford.

Beware!

Always beware of uncovered losses. Ask your insurance professional to explain to you what is, and what is not covered, with any insurance you purchase. It is common that some losses are not covered. For example, seldom are losses by flooding covered under regular policies. To get this coverage, you need typically to purchase flood insurance.

Liability Insurance Coverage

You also need to consider purchasing liability insurance coverage. Unlike insurance that protects your property, you need insurance against the risk of being sued if you cause injury or property damage to someone else. For example, if

Check the Policy

If you're operating a freelance graphic design business from your home, your homeowner's insurance is not likely to cover any liability losses. Most homeowner's policies specifically exempt losses from any business endeavors. Your business equipment is also typically not covered. Contact your insurance professional to discuss the gap in coverage. In some cases, a homeowner's policy can be amended to provide the coverage you need. In other cases, you will need a separate insurance policy to insure you properly against potential losses.

you are renting office space and someone trips, falls on a rug in your office, and is injured, he might sue you for compensation for his pain and suffering, medical bills, and lost wages. To protect yourself against this type of claim, you transfer the risk to an insurance company.

In today's litigious society, liability insurance is not a luxury, but a necessity. Make sure your insurance professional fully understands what your business is and what you do as part of your routine business activities. The last thing you ever want is to suffer a loss and hear the words "Sorry, you're not covered."

Health Care

Health care is a thorny issue these days, and is one of those items that you are going to need to purchase. Whether your freelance graphic design business consists of just you or multiple employees, health care and insuring for the costs associated with it are part of business today.

Sometimes, hospitalization insurance can be purchased through group policies available for business associations or organizations. You might find more reasonably priced hospitalization coverage from professional associations, your chamber of commerce, or directly from health insurance providers.

Tax Liabilities

It doesn't take long before you are facing specific tax liabilities. For example, if you are required to collect sales tax, those funds you collect are not yours, but rather the taxing authority's. You might be required to place those funds in a special escrow account, or you may only need to turn them in when you file a return or collection report.

Obviously, you must have the funds available to pay taxes when they are due. This may require you to set up additional bank accounts or use some other method to keep your tax liability funds available for payment when due.

Your tax liabilities could also include:

- Social Security taxes
- Self-employment taxes
- Medicare tax
- Local income taxes
- Federal employee taxes
- State income taxes

Be sure to keep your tax liability funds separate and available for payment when due.

Workers' Compensation

If you have an employee, you must have workers' compensation insurance. Workers' compensation insurance covers employees who are injured while performing their job duties during their employment.

The purpose of workers' compensation is to avoid lawsuits by employees against employers. The idea is that employees get their medical bills and lost wages paid, and give up the right to sue their employers. As you can imagine, it doesn't work well for the employee-employer relationship when the employee sues the employer. Also, it could take years to get a case through the courts. Workers' compensation is a no-fault system. The goal is to get the employee the medical attention needed without needing to prove negligence or fault of the employer in causing the injury.

Smart Tip

You must have workers' compensation on yourself if you are an employee of your own corporation. In some areas, you may be able to waive this requirement if you are the sole employee of your own corporation.

In the vast majority of states, workers' compensation is provided solely by private insurance companies. In 12 states, the state government operates a state fund. Some states allow workers' compensation coverage through private insurers or a state fund. State funds are generally required to act as assigned-risk programs or insurers of last resort. They only underwrite workers' compensation policies.

In contrast, private insurers can turn away the worst risks. They can write comprehensive insurance packages, which include general liability, natural disasters, and so on. The largest state fund is California's State Compensation Insurance Fund. The federal government pays its workers' compensation obligations for its own employees through regular appropriations.

Your insurance professional can advise you on what type of workers' compensation plans are available for you in your state. Graphic design is classified as a low-risk profession, and accordingly, you should enjoy low rates.

Fun Fact

Originally known as *workmens' compensation*, today most have adopted the term *workers' compensation* as a gender-neutral name.

Expanding Your Freelance Graphic Design Business

Congratulations! Your freelance graphic design business is a success! You've got some clients, you're creating designs, you're enjoying the work, and most importantly, you're making money. Life is good. Congratulations.

But now what? Where do you go from here? That's the question this chapter attempts to answer.

As a freelance graphic designer, you have a lot of freedom to go in other directions and try new things. That freedom to do what you want is probably one of the reasons you decided to become a freelancer in the first place.

Other Profitable Sidelines

One of the things you might try are other profitable sidelines that you could offer to your customers. By doing so, you can make yourself more valuable to your clients.

Sometimes sidelines take off, and change your whole approach to your business. Many times this happens without a lot of planning, while other times it is part of a well-thought-out approach to expanding your business.

Offering Additional Services to Your Clients

Your clients often will ask you about additional services or want you to complete work that you are not prepared to take on. When this happens repeatedly, it usually signals a need (on the part of your current clients) and a great opportunity to make additional money.

Consider a hypothetical client with whom you have a good working relationship. Your client has asked you to design a newsletter, and you delivered the work. Then the client comes back to you and asks if you can edit the newsletter. That is not within the realm of what your graphic design business does. So you turn down the work.

But why shouldn't you start offering editorial services in addition to graphic design services? You could easily contract out the editorial work out to local freelance writers and editors, and quickly your freelance graphic design business has expanded.

Yours may only make $5 or $10 per billed hour (you charge your client $40 an hour and you pay your freelance editor $35 per hour). You aren't going to get rich, but you are going to maintain a good relationship with your client. Your client is going to be looking elsewhere for the editorial service, and perhaps stumble across another graphic designer that can deliver the complete package. Keeping clients happy and providing the services they want is a sure way to maintain the business relationship.

> **Tip...**
>
> **Smart Tip**
>
> "It's a competitive business but don't give up," advises Baltimore-based graphic designer Sharon Reuter. "Persevere. Work hard, meet deadlines, and don't burn any bridges along the way."

What Are You Selling Now?

Take a good look at what you are selling now. Most likely it is graphic design, and mostly in a given area. When you think about it, it won't take much for you to expand. You could, from designing newsletters, offer all kinds of extra services:

- Proofreading
- Editing
- Writing
- E-mail newsletter creation

Some graphic designers go further by specializing in a specific design area. For example, if they are specializing in newsletters, they take on the entire process, and become a newsletter factory, even mailing and/or delivering the newsletter. They become a true one-stop shop for their clients and prospects. And sometimes this kind of sideline takes over and becomes the entire graphic design business.

This type of specialization can provide vast new opportunities for you and your work. Specialization, as in this example from newsletter design, could make you a leading competitor in your marketplace. Don't overlook how specialization, sometimes started as a sideline to your regular design work, can grow your freelance graphic design business.

One of the other benefits you can offer clients is the simple service of just keeping them on schedule. For those not used to working with deadlines, projects often slip. This is true with newsletter production, website updates, and other similar projects.

Specializing in Newsletter Production

Newsletters are something that many organizations and companies want, but don't realize the work involved in creating them. Often the hardest part is to decide what to include in the newsletter. This is where you can act as a newsletter consultant, moving your clients beyond just pictures of employees and praise for their company. They need to create an effective communication tool that is of interest to their clients and prospects, and not just details of interest only to their staff.

▲

Selling to Publications

Another area where you can expand your freelance graphic design business is into publications. Publishers often need the services of a graphic artists or designers. Publisher routinely produce books or magazines, or other specialized materials. While they often have designers on staff, their staff often is occupied with other projects. So don't hesitate to contact publishers and offer your services.

Desktop Publishing Services

As a graphic designer, you might (or might not) be offering desktop publishing services. It depends what you call *desktop publishing* and most importantly, what *your clients* call desktop publishing.

A Chicago graphic designer practically doubled his graphic design business just by letting his current client base know that he would accept desktop publishing business. It wasn't a term he was using because he thought it meant a lesser-level of design expertise to many people. However, his clients wanted what they know as desktop publishing. Just by alerting his clients that he could complete publishing of manuals, books, and newsletters, his business doubled within three months. Even though his design work is far beyond the person with only rudimentary desktop publishing skills, by describing the work he could do in a way his clients understood, he improved his business dramatically.

> ### Smart Tip
> *Tip...*
>
> "You need to know if you are the type of person who can work alone," Ann Arbor, Michigan's Mary Cronin says. With 12 years of experience as a graphic designer, she says, "Sometimes it can feel very isolating. A pet helps. You also have to have good time management skills. It is amazing what can distract you, like the refrigerator!"

Improving Your Designs

Another way to expand your business is to improve your design capability, which might require additional training or education on your part. It might also mean that you have to acquire additional equipment so you can deliver a different finished product to your customer. For example, you decide to move into computer animation, but to do so, you need a new computer and software. In addition, you need to learn how to use this new tool once you have it installed and set up in your office.

Change and new tools are natural evolutions in the design business. There is and will always be change. Consider websites. Two decades ago, no one knew what a website would look and feel like, and today, everyone needs one. Those who employ the services of a professional graphic designer have the better-looking sites. While a programmer might be able to set up a site so it works, the look and feel is often horrendous. You, as a freelance graphic designer, cannot sit back and wait. Often, you must be in the forefront of change.

This can open up additional career paths or opportunities for you. Leading the way in a new technology could present the opportunity for you to teach others, which furthers your credibility, knowledge, and skills, and helps in your overall marketing efforts.

Designing on Speculation

Always keeping busy is a big part of operating a success freelance graphic design business. When not marketing in the slow times, consider designing on speculation. Using your target-marketing list, create a new design or graphic, and show it to the potential client. This "makeover" is a good way to highlight your talents and skills. It also keeps the creative juices flowing and you busy.

Working on speculation is a good way to develop additional skills. You may, for example, want to work more as an illustrator. In this area of graphic design, people focus more on drawing, painting, and creating computer-generated artwork. Graphic artists often utilize illustrations in their designs, so developing additional illustration skills could expand your business.

The demand for graphic designers with web design skills is on the rise. As a web designer, you integrate your traditional graphic art skills with web technology. If you are not getting your share of this business, consider expanding into it.

> **Bright Idea**
> Consider the makeover as a "free sample," but you don't need to give the design to the potential client. If working on speculation does not open the door for additional work, keep your makeover design as part of your portfolio to show other potential clients.

Working on "spec," is an area of contention among graphic designers. Some refuse to work on "pitches" or do graphic designs on speculation. "I do not participate in spec-work or pitches. It's bad for graphic designers to participate in this type of business development strategy," says Los Angeles-based Pertrula Vrontikis. "The graphic design industry doesn't pitch for million-dollar accounts like an agency, or for assignments that last three to five years, like an architectural firm. Our work is primarily per project, so the reward is not worth the gamble."

Education and Training

If you need additional training or education in a new or unfamiliar area, take the time to enhance your skills. It doesn't take long to be left behind in today's technology. Re-tool and keep yourself current with your professional development.

Some people prefer to learn on their own, by experimentation, and through trial and error. Others read books. Some learn faster and better in a classroom environment. It doesn't matter how you learn, but what does matter is that you take time to learn new technologies and methods. Don't overlook how important it is for you to continue your professional development.

"Reflecting on the past, one of the challenges an established firm has over the years is staying creatively current in the industry," says Petrula Vrontikis. "I have tried to resolve this by an on-going commitment to teaching. It has helped me refine my ability to communicate ideas, and help others do the same. My students help keep me current on trends in their world. Teaching informs my practice, and my practice lends credibility to my teaching."

"All of this was unexpected, and has made my career quite fulfilling," Vrontikis says. "I often hire students that I admire and who I feel would integrate well into the Vrontikis Design office chemistry. Sixty percent of my full-time and freelance design staff have been former students from Art Center. I understand and trust the process they went through there and know what it says about their level of care, dedication, and stamina."

Expand Your Design Business with E-Mail

As a graphic designer, you can use e-mail to expand your marketing effort. Ilise Benun, the Hoboken, New Jersey-based marketing consultant to graphic designers, says that you should use e-mail as a targeted marketing method. "You begin by sending individual messages to prospects as part of a cold-calling campaign and as a way of introducing yourself and your services to them," Benun advises. "Once you have a dialogue going, you ask if you can stay in touch by e-mail. Once they agree, you get them into your loop and send them your e-mail newsletter monthly or quarterly."

Benun says that an e-mail marketing campaign—sending regular e-mail messages to everyone you know and everyone who knows you—is one of the best ways to market your services because it can consistently accomplish many things at once. "It can showcase your creativity, increase your visibility, and build credibility, while also distinguishing you from the competition. Plus, it's the best way to drive traffic to your website; it's much more reliable and targeted than the search engines," Benun says.

To avoid being perceived as a spammer, you must create an e-mail message that people want to receive and that is unlike anything else they receive. To do that, you must:

1. Know your market well. If they're small business owners, you send something different than what you'd send to corporate types.

2. Send material and ideas that your market and network finds useful and that is relevant to their situation.

3. Use your own voice and let your personality come through your messages.

Here are some ideas from Benun as to what to send:

- *Case studies and real-life examples.* Your prospects love to see what others like them are doing. That's why they will take time to read a simple case study that describes a problem you solved for a client. Showing how you've helped clients address specific challenges is good from a promotional perspective, too, because it gives concrete examples of the work you do, which can otherwise seem abstract.

- *Offer a list of your top three to five tips on a subject.* Think about what type of hints you can give your clients and prospects about how to make the process of working with you go smoothly. Turn these hints into tips, like "How to Hire a Designer" or "How to Get Great Work from a Designer."

- *Answer your clients' frequently-asked questions.* Keep track of the questions your clients ask, whether via e-mail or in person. Then answer each in a short article. If you can't think of any questions, send your current clients a quick message asking for their questions.

- *Offer your opinion on a hot topic.* Don't be afraid to tackle the hot issues in your field. Offer your own expert opinion. Your readers want to know.

"You also don't have to create all the content from scratch," Benun says. "You can simply pass along links to articles that would be of interest to your market or to websites they might find interesting or inspiring."

Printing and Reprography Service

Graphic designers can develop additional profits by offering reprographics or commercial printing services. Any items regularly produced for businesses or associations by commercial job printers can be profitably supplied and delivered by graphic designers. Sometimes called *reprographics* or *print brokering*, you offer products much as if you were a commercial printer. Reprography is the reproduction of graphics through mechanical means, such as photography or xerography. Reprography is often used in catalogs or archives, as well as in the engineering, architectural, and construction industries.

With today's technology and industry standards, getting started is easy. Graphic designers have a real competitive edge over others in this field because of their design skills.

This additional service allows graphic designers to advertise or offer special rates and prices for printing. The types of items vary:

- Business cards
- Envelopes
- Letterheads
- Invoices
- Statements
- Brochures
- Presentation folders
- Signs
- Fliers

- Calendars
- Books
- Booklets
- Catalogs
- Labels
- Posters
- Rubber stamps
- Continuous forms
- Postcards

As a graphic designer offering printing services, you have two options:

1. creating or producing the items yourself, or

2. processing an order and sending it to a commercial printer.

Both options are available to graphic designers who wish to enter this lucrative field. The concept is simple: to attract graphic design clients, you offer a printed product. For example, you might offer 1,000 business cards for $20. As businesses come forward with orders, you offer graphic design services for the cards and other items they may need.

Creating Products

One of your two options is to create items yourself and deliver them to clients. You could, for example, purchase a commercial printing press, paper cutter, and other expensive items that would allow you to produce business cards. As part of your services, you could offer design services for the business cards.

This is simply not practical, however. Few business people would consider purchasing all the equipment necessary to produce business cards. Most become dealers and sell business cards for another printer.

In today's world, technology has made it easy to reproduce or manufacture some items. What is known as an office photocopier can often produce large numbers of copies. This allows the reproduction of brochures. Today's hardware can produce full color copies.

Other products that can easily be produced by graphic designers are signs and banners. Equipment needs vary, depending on the type of products that are being created for customers. A wide-format printer, sign software, cutting tools, and some vinyl supplies are what it takes to offer this service. These kinds of signs are used at trade shows and special events. As a graphic designer, you can not only deliver the signs but also create logos and art used for promotion.

> **Tip...**
>
> **Smart Tip**
> Many office equipment suppliers offer monthly rental contracts. This eliminates the need for a major financial investment in equipment.

Finding Equipment

Searches on the internet allow you to locate suppliers and equipment easily. Simple searches in the search engines can generate hundreds of possible vendors that can provide equipment and supplies. Many companies offer free consulting or advice to help you get started. Used and new equipment can also often be located on eBay. Supplies are also just as easy to locate online, but you may want to find local suppliers that offer free shipping or next-day delivery.

Getting Training

Depending on the type of products or services you want to offer, training could be informal or extensive. Learning to become a full-fledged commercial printer could take years. That is, of course, beyond the scope of this book. But learning to operate a special printer or computer software might only take an afternoon of informal learning and some practice. Vendors often offer training and provide free telephone support.

Wholesale Printing

Another option to enter this lucrative business is to become a dealer or reseller of commercial printing. Samples or catalogs are your selling tools. You take the order, collect the money, and turn in an order. Your commission can range from 10 to 50 percent of the order.

The benefits of becoming a dealer include:

- Easy to offer profitable product lines
- No inventory to carry

95

▲

- Quality printing
- Fast delivery
- Online sales opportunities

Sometimes called *print brokering*, wholesale printing has long been an established practice in the printing industry. Because of their substantial investments in specific printing presses and equipment, printers have offered "discounts to the trade." This means that others can purchase printing at a wholesale rate. It's done to keep the printing press rolling and producing income.

The trade discount is offered to dealers. In other words, these specialized printers have two price lists: a retail price list and a wholesale one. A printing broker is an order taker for one or more commercial printers. You take orders for anything from business cards to circulars to large printing orders, take your agreed upon commission, and then pass on the order to the printer. Many jobs are small, but they can be quite large and expensive, such as a full-color catalog.

Fun Fact

Many of the business card "printers" you find on the internet are not printers, but dealers. They are simply filling orders for major printing companies.

It is rather easy to become an approved dealer. You need little more than a sales tax or reseller certificate from your state's taxing authority and a business card. After completing a simple application, you become an approved dealer. Some companies may charge a nominal amount for a sample package or album, and often any deposit is refunded on your first order.

Many dealer programs require advance payment to receive the discounted price. This is easy for the graphic designer to do. You simply collect the printing payment from your customer, deduct your discount or commission, and send the balance to your printer.

Depending on the company you are working with as a dealer, you may never see the printed product. The printer drop ships the order directly to your customer. You receive a sample of the finished item, along with your invoice.

Locating Printers

There are several ways to locate printers who offer trade discounts. The fastest way to find wholesale printers is to search for them on the internet. The keywords "wholesale printing" will produce many different results. Adding the type of printing you want to sell such as "wholesale business card printing," will produce more specific results.

Here are four of the many commercial printers that are currently operating a wholesale printing program:

1. *Beyer Printing Inc.*
   1855 Air Lane Drive
   Nashville, TN 37210
   Toll free: (800) 256-4948
   www.buyerprinting.com

2. *GR Print & Marketing Services Inc.*
   1528 Highland Avenue
   Duarte, CA 91010
   Toll free: (877) 774-6818
   www.grprint.com

3. *Horton Printing*
   P.O. Box 46
   515 West College Street
   Fayetteville, TN 37334
   Toll free (888) 495-8031
   www.hortonprinting.com

4. *Regency Thermographers*
   P.O Box 508
   Waynesboro, PA 17268-0508
   Toll free: 1-87REGENCY1
   www.regencythermo.com

Bright Idea
You can also find printers by reading trade magazines for the graphic arts industry. Printers often advertise in the magazines.

Marketing the Business

Strategies for marketing the reprographics or printing products are easily devised. For most graphic designers who do enter this area, one or two products are heavily promoted at a discount price.

One graphic designer, based in suburban Philadelphia, agreed to be interviewed for this book, but requested her name not be used. She started in a sideline in business cards 11 years ago, and it still thrives today. At the time, she offered 1,000 business cards for $7. Today, the price is $18 per 1,000. These are no-frills cards. But it is enough to make her telephone ring. She used, and still uses, small classified ads. One of her favorite advertising vehicles are those small, weekly advertising papers that are delivered. Ads cost only $15 to $20 per week.

Her overall strategy was as simple then as it is now. She wanted to sell her logo creation service. She thought the best way to find this business was to offer business cards at a discount so start-up businesses would seek her out. Although she never expected to make any money selling business cards, she turned a reasonable profit.

"Finding my suppliers allowed me to make 40 percent on each order," she says. "It doesn't sound like much, but there have been weeks when I processed over 300 business card orders."

The profit margin increases as cards with multicolors are purchased. One week, a real estate office with over 100 agents ordered special cards that needed gold stamping. She was able to capture the order, and made more than $2,500.

One of her friends is a nearby printing broker that took this concept one step further. She opened a storefront, which consisted of nothing much more than a table, some chairs, and a counter. Located on a busy road, she became a printing broker by selling five-cent photocopies. A sign along the edge of the road attracted people who stopped to use her photocopier.

She sold all kinds of printing, from wedding invitations to invoices. With the exception of filling her copying machine with paper and fluid, she never operated or owned a printing press.

"I don't like to say much about my business," she confided in an e-mail. "Most of my customers think I have a printing company and presses. I never said I do, or don't. I just fill their orders. Because I selected my printers carefully, I never have a quality issue."

She did admit that she got started in the printing brokering business by accident. "I had a client who sold advertising on placemats that were given to diners," she said. "I did the layout and design of the small ads. His printer was getting very expensive, and he asked me to find or recommend someone else. So I started to call around, and was asked if I wanted a "trade discount." At the time, I had no idea what that even meant. But I was able to make $150 extra on each menu preparation job, so I started print brokering."

Beware!
Get your money up front before you place an order. Because printing is customized and can't be sold elsewhere, make sure your customer pays you.

Her business grew from there. Then the decision to rent a small storefront came. "I had enough business that I knew I could make it, but I was relying on the five-cent copies to really boost my walk-in traffic. That worked."

She has several photocopiers now, and does stock colored and specialized papers for special customer requests. She gives away free coffee and keeps her shop open later in the evening for wedding customers.

"I am kind of competing with Kinkos and those fast copy shops attached to the big stationery stores," she says. "But I am able to do more, and offer really good customer service."

This entrepreneur says she doesn't do much graphic design work. "I was never a real graphic designer," she admits. "I just learned to do typesetting and had a knack for it. I had a couple of clients, and one needed some extra help. I helped out, and it was the beginning of my print brokering business."

11

The Secrets of
Designing
Success

Managing your freelance graphic design business takes effort. It won't happen by itself. One of the reasons why you wanted to start your own enterprise and not be an employee of another is to manage your own career. But you do need to stop design work from time to time to manage your business.

▲

The management of your business requires your attention. You have decisions to make. Some you will regret. Others will make sense, and you'll be glad you decided the way you did. One graphic designer from Milwaukee said on a message forum that he regretted not taking the time to speak to sales representative about a payroll service. After paying a penalty for not filing forms on time, he finally took the time out of his schedule and met with the representative. "From that point forward, it has worked out perfectly. They take care of everything, from completing the forms, writing payroll checks, issuing the W2s. Why I didn't do this earlier, I don't know!"

That kind of management, taking care of details, is part of what you need to do to operate your freelance graphic design business successfully.

Setting Your Fees

One of the questions that will repeatedly surface as you work as a freelance graphic designer is, "How much should I charge for design?" It is the most common question asked by freelancers. It is also one of the most difficult to answer. There are many factors to consider before coming to a decision.

No one answer covers all the bases. Some of the following categories are typical factors to be taken into account when deciding how much to

> **Tip...**
>
> **Smart Tip**
> When a client wants a fixed-rate estimate, deliver it with a range, such as $1,200 to $1,450. This gives you some leeway, and allows you to bill more or less within the range, depending on the actual time it takes to complete the work.

charge a client. These are only guidelines. In reality, freelance graphic designers should research carefully and develop a pricing structure best suited to their own business.

1. *Experience.* How much experience does the designer have and what have they got to offer? Obviously, a creative director with 30 years experience will be able to command a higher fee than a college leaver. And a brand identity formulated by a well-known design group that needs to pay for account handlers and offices will cost a lot more than a logo designed by a self-employed graphic designer working in a home office.

2. *Type of work.* Many graphic designers charge different rates depending on the type of work. This occurs even if this work is part of the same job for the same client. For example, conceptual work often is charged at a higher rate than production work. They approach this as if they were working for a large agency. Work that a senior designer would do is billed at a higher rate than work than a junior staffer would complete.

3. *Location.* Graphic design rates vary drastically depending on the location of the designer. This can often be an advantage for graphic designers who work

remotely and maintain clients in bigger cities. Market rates—the standard rates—are often a range. For example, a graphic designer rate might be $50 to $75 per hour in one region. In another, the normal rates might be $65 to $85 per hour. Location can determine the going rate.

4. *Web design.* Multimedia, Flash, and other interactive design work is generally more expensive than static HTML page design. The conceptual stages of the design project may take up a large part of the costs. The project management portion of the web design may also be a significant part of the final project.

5. *The client.* What to charge for a graphic design assignment also depends on the client. The value of the project is not just dependent on the amount of work that a graphic designer has to put into it. It is also depends on the value that the final design will bring to the client. This is often dependent on the client's spending power. Some graphic designers will adjust their design fees. A major corporation expects to pay more than a small business or a non-profit.

6. *Loss-leaders, pro bono, free pitching.* Graphic designers debate how much free work they should do for a client. Some take part in this process. Many designers refuse to take part in free pitching for work. Loss-leaders are also a controversial area. Some graphic designers suggest that it is necessary to pitch with low fees for the initial job from a client. They say that is the best way to draw in a new client. Others graphic designers argue that a client that expects a cheap job once will continue to do so.

7. *Creative versus standard work.* Most graphic designers have found that designs that push the creative boundaries are rarely the ones that pay the best. Designers may well find that a standard yet boring financial report for a corporate client pays better than an award-winning, interactive Flash presentation.

It is also important to estimate for and pass on the costs of other expenses, such as photography, picture research, travel, and other similar expenses. Designers bill these associated design costs in many different ways, but they all have to be paid.

Formulas, Hourly Rates, or Flat Fees?

There are numerous guides and business plans that aim to provide freelance graphic

> **Bright Idea**
>
> If you are going to accept work from clients that requires you to work extraordinary hours or over the weekend, you might as well get paid extra for doing it. Don't feel bad or apologize for charging more. Clients do understand and expect that they must pay more for people to work weekends or late into the night. You should charge a premium rate for this type of off-hours work.

designers with methods for calculating how much to charge clients. Some are more useful and realistic than others. But, when it comes to setting your graphic design rates, it often comes down to experience. Even the most carefully planned job can quickly go over budget. At the same time, a job that was expected to last a week can sometimes be completed in a few hours. These are all factors that need to be considered when deciding which method of costing a design job to adopt.

Smart Tip Tip...

Need more help? The Small Business Administration (SBA) has online tutorials about price setting and sample business plans for you to check out. Go to www.sbaonline.sba.gov/ starting/indexbusplans.html.

One of the best methods of research is to find out how other designers go about working out how much to charge for design work. Some clients are fee-conscious, while others are not. Some prefer an hourly rate, while others want a fixed-cost fee. You will find some clients would rather you bill by the hour and will not question your time. Others will scrutinize your time and expense invoices under a microscope. Other clients that prefer a flat rate know you will pad the time just to cover extra time or work, but prefer that method, knowing the fixed-rate is their cost for the project. The key is to be flexible, sensible, and profitable.

Pricing Strategies

There are various pricing strategies. Most are based on a per hour rate. For example, you might charge $60 per hour for your graphic design work. However, your rate might be multiplied 1½ to 2 times for 24-hour rush service (a-time-and-half-rate) when a client wants the work done and turned around immediately. For jobs requiring weekend work, your rate is doubled.

It's really your decision as to what you will bill per hour and what extra you will charge if you are asked to work late into the wee hours of next morning or to give up a weekend.

If you go with this type of fee setting, your rate sheet would like something like this:

Graphic design	$60 per hour (normal rate)
Assignments requiring 24-hour turnaround (RUSH) or work after normal business hours	1½ times the normal rate
Assignments requiring weekend work (Saturday and/or Sunday)	2 times the normal rate

If you don't charge extra for off-hours work, your clients may learn they can take advantage of you and assign work over the weekends or work that they want back the next day, no matter how long you have to work through the night to get it done. To stop this type of abuse, set a policy where you charge more for these types of assignments. You may still get the assignments, but you are going to be a lot happier doing the work knowing you are being paid at a higher rate.

Planning and Handling Downtime

There are times when you have work for which you cannot bill a client. Some of the activities that require your attention or time and that are not billable include:

- Training and education
- Marketing
- Accounting (bill paying, issuing invoices to clients, receiving payments)
- Errands (going to the bank, post office, etc.)
- Office and computer maintenance

Keep this in mind when setting your fees, too. A percentage of your time cannot be billable because of other important duties. If your goal is to bill 40 hours per week, for 50 weeks per year, the total billable hours are 2,000. At $50 per hour, you have billed $100,000. Of course, you have not included downtime or time for those activities that you must do. At $60 per hour, the total billable time would deliver $120,000. This higher rate gives you the ability to take the time to manage your business, and even though you would not bill 2,000 hours, you could still hit your goal of billing $100,000.

> **Tip...**
>
> **Smart Tip**
> Always plan for some downtime in your schedule. At the least, you will want (and need) to take some vacation and holidays away from work.

Outsourcing

One way to minimize nonbillable hours is to outsource some of the work you must do. One freelancer always stopped working on projects at noon on Fridays and spent the remainder of the day reorganizing and cleaning her office. Then it hit her: she could hire a cleaning person to do this work. She paid $80 for the work, but she could bill for four more hours. Her rate—$75 per hour—meant that she could pay $80 to bill $300. Plus, she did not have to do work that she did not enjoy and could do the work that she likes doing. "Why didn't I think of this sooner?" she asks herself.

Consider outsourcing as much as your work as you can, especially those chores that must be done but can't be squeezed easily into your schedule. Some are obvious: cleaning, payroll services, accounting, and other ordinary business activities.

▲

It may not seem like much on the surface, but if you could eliminate four hours of nonbillable time each week, over a year, that's 200 hours. And at $50 per hour, that totals $10,000. Even if you paid $5,000 for someone else to do those services for you, you'd still be ahead by $5,000.

Managing the Marketing

You must maintain your marketing efforts, even when you are busy. If you don't, you could find yourself not having enough work in the future. Many freelancers overlook this important step, but they should maintain their marketing continuously to ensure future profitability.

Because they get busy—that's the nature freelancing—they slack off the marketing plan. At the time, it might make sense. But later, it proves disastrous. Once projects are finished, they begin to market again. Nevertheless, there is often a lull before more work is located. That translates to nonbillable time and loss of income.

Keep Planning Your Business

As you learned earlier in this book, a business plan is critical to your success. You learned to create one—and follow it. As your business progresses and you become successful and profitable, it is all too likely that you may stop referring to your plan, allowing it to sit on a shelf. This is not smart.

Getting Started When Employment Ends

Karen Billipp never planned to be a graphic designer. It just turned out that way.

"I actually started in publishing 20 years ago as an editorial assistant," Karen says. "I worked for a small publisher, which meant I got to do EVERYTHING from author contracts to art paste up."

In her do-everything job, Karen soon discovered what she like doing the best. "I found that I was interested in the design of books and the best way to convey the information through thoughtful design," she says. "Enter the computer. As the computer started expanding into the publishing arena, so did my skills in using it. I have never had formal training in graphic design, but have picked up ideas

Getting Started When Employment Ends, continued

and techniques while on the job. I have also attended various workshops, but basically I am self-taught."

Then, things changed. Karen was working for a small publisher that was bought by a larger one. "The company was moving to the Midwest, and I was not interested in going. I had three years experience in desktop publishing and design, my reputation was solid, and I didn't want to look for another job that would grant me the flexibility I needed. I also must add that the opportunities in this locale were limited," Karen explains. "I decided to start my own business and was able to acquire the company that bought the one I worked for as my first client."

Today, Karen works from her home office located in the hamlet of Eliot, Maine. As with most freelancers, she has to balance her workflow. "One challenge is deciding when I have enough work. As a freelancer, I never want to say no to anyone. Unfortunately, that can backfire with having too much work," Karen says. "It is very difficult finding a good balance with the level of work."

Another challenge is time. "It is all related to the amount of work I accept, but I find I am working harder than I ever have for an employer. Part of it is my reputation and my desire to uphold it and the other is the amount of work," she says.

"Another challenge, though it is just the nature of the business, is keeping up with new software programs. It seems that some of the software needs updating annually. Hardware is usually updated every two years," Karen says. "Because my work revolves around the computer, it is essential that I stay current in all aspects of my field."

Karen doesn't offer a wide array of graphic services because the focus of her graphic design business is book production. She designs the book layouts and has done some book covers and logo work, but the bulk of her business is managing the "birth" of a book—taking it from manuscript through all the production phases to sending a CD to the printer.

When asked what advice she would give to other graphic designers who want to be their own boss, Karen says, "I would advise people to do it. It is so satisfying to work for yourself as long as you are goal-oriented and disciplined. I have an office in my house and there are times when I would rather wash the dishes than tackle the latest project. It takes a lot of self-discipline to make me sit down and focus. There are always distractions, which you must learn to avoid. It is a great feeling to be in business for yourself."

Karen, who has enough business that she doesn't have a web site, operates under the name of Eliot House Productions. And she enjoys the freedom of

▲

Getting Started When Employment Ends, continued

being a self-employed graphic designer. "I love the fact that I don't have to go to staff meetings or waste time commuting. I love being able to head off to my son's soccer game at 3:30 in the afternoon. I end up having to make up the time I am away, but it means I have the freedom to choose what is important to me," Karen says.

Moving from employee to self-employed also meant making adjustments in the way she works and manages her business. "I realized there was no mail room, no amenities, and that I would have to do all this myself—order supplies, do my own shipping, etc. I am also my own IT staff, though I do have someone I can call when things get really confusing," she explains.

"The other thing I kind of forgot about was taxes. I would receive payment for a job thinking I had made a bunch of money! Then I was educated to the quarterly tax payments I have to make during the year. It is based on your previous year's income. So, you always have to keep that in mind as a freelancer," Billipp says. "Otherwise, I think I was well prepared for having my own business due to growing up with an entrepreneurial father."

You should revise and update your plan. At a minimum of every six months, you should review it and make decisions of what to change, add, or remove from your plan. Then, of course, you should implement those changes in your business.

By reviewing your business plan, and keeping it current, you might decide to

- add additional web design services,
- create informational products,
- add employees (additional designers), and/or
- add new hardware/software.

No matter what you decide, methodic planning always makes sense. Always maintain your business plan. Keep it current and actively modify it. Don't allow it to become dormant.

Not as Lonely as You Think

Although you will spend many hours at your workstation producing work for your clients, it doesn't have to be as lonely as it might first appear. Whether working from your home office or rented space used as your design studio, there are always opportunities for you to get out and be among peers and potential clients, such as chamber of commerce meetings, graphic design organizations, seminars, and workshops.

Take the time to attend the mixers and meetings. Socialize, and let people get to know you, too. Don't go to meetings and be quiet. Get involved and connect with others in attendance. Remember that they are there to learn, find out what is happening in the graphic design industry, and to meet and network with others. They are there to meet you, too.

All areas have some kind of art director or graphic designer association. It may take a little digging because the names vary, but there will be these kinds of organizations. Find the one closest to you, and become an active part of the organization.

"Don't just join, but actively participate in graphic design organizations such as the AIGA," says Petrula Vrontikis, a graphic designer in Los Angeles. "Enter competitions and attend events and conferences. Make your studio a desirable place to work by creating great design opportunities and providing a terrific environment. You and your staff will enjoy being there each day."

Success and Design On, or Stop

There are a number of warning signs that you may not be cut out to operate a freelance graphic design business. Failing to complete your work on time and by deadline, not making enough money, working long and difficult hours, or not having the time or money for vacations are just some of the signs that things are not going as planned. And let's face it, if you are not a happy person, your design work will not be creative, crisp, or fresh. Unhappy designers usually do lousy or haphazard work. You might be able to put on the happy face to your clients, but the work will still be lacking.

"Being the boss, is one the three best things about being a self-employed graphic artist," Petrula Vrontikis says. She also says that, "being the boss" is one of the worst things about being self-employed. "When things are bad, it's your fault."

That sentiment was echoed by fellow graphic artist and designer Brent Almond, who adds, "Always the bottom line, [you are the] one responsible if anything goes wrong."

You always have the option of seeking regular employment. You might need a mentor, particularly one that could help you with either time management or marketing. Don't overlook the fact that you might need to offer something different to the market. Tweaking what you are offering to design could make all the difference.

▲

Only you can decide if things are not going as planned. A failed business venture is not the end of the world. You will have learned important lessons and skills, which you can use in the future. Hopefully, your freelance graphic design business will be wildly successful. Good luck!

Appendix A
Sample Contracts and Agreements

The following are sample contracts and agreements for you to use as examples. Please consult with legal counsel to make sure a contract or agreement is of benefit to you.

▲

Sample Collaboration Contract

AGREEMENT entered into as of this _____ day of _____, 20___, between
_____ (hereinafter referred to as the "Graphic Artist"), located at
_____, and _____
(hereinafter referred to as the "Co-Graphic Artist"), located at _____
_____.

WHEREAS, each party is familiar with and respects the work of the other; and,

WHEREAS, the parties hereto wish to collaborate on a graphic arts or design project tentatively titled _____ (hereinafter referred to as the "Work"); and WHEREAS, the parties wish to have the creation of the Work governed by the mutual obligations, covenants, and conditions herein;

NOW, THEREFORE, in consideration of the foregoing premises and the mutual covenants hereinafter set forth and other valuable considerations, the parties hereto agree as follows:

Description. The Work shall be _____
_____
_____. Materials other than text include _____
_____
_____
_____.

A [ ] schedule [ ] outline [ ] synopsis is attached to and made part of this agreement.

Responsibilities. The Graphic Artist shall be responsible for creating _____
_____
_____
_____.

The Graphic Artist shall also provide the following materials _____
_____
_____
_____
_____.

The Co-Graphic Artist shall be responsible for writing approximately _____ words to serve as the following parts of the text _____
_____
_____
_____.

The Co-Graphic Artist shall also provide the following materials _____
_____
_____
_____.

Due Date. Both Graphic Artist and Co-Graphic Artist shall complete their portions of the Work by _____, 20 _____, or by the date for delivery of the project as specified in a production contract entered into pursuant to Paragraph 4. If such a production contract requires sketches or other materials prior to the date for delivery of the project, the party responsible for same shall provide it to the client. In the event either party fails to complete his or her portion of the Work by the due date for reasons other than death or disability, the parties may agree to an extension of the due date or agree to allow a nondefaulting party to complete the Work as if the other party were deceased or disabled. If no agreement can be reached, the arbitrator may award a nondefaulting party the right to complete the Work as if the other party were deceased or disabled or may convey to each party the rights of copyright in that party's completed portion of the Work and specify how the parties shall contribute to any expenses incurred and repay any advances.

Contracts and Licenses. If a contract for the Work has not already been entered into with a client, both Graphic Artist and Co-Graphic Artist agree to seek such a contract. Such production contract shall be entered into in the names of and signed by both the Graphic Artist and the Co-Graphic Artist, each of whom shall comply with and perform all required contractual obligations. If a mutually agreeable production contract for initial publication of the Work is not entered into with a client by _____, 20_____, then either party may terminate this agreement by giving written notice to the other party prior to such time as a mutually agreeable production contract for initial publication is entered into. Each party shall fully inform the other party of all negotiations for such a production contract or with respect to the negotiation of any other licenses or contracts pursuant to this Agreement. The disposition of any right, including the grant of any license, shall require written agreement between both parties hereto. Each party shall receive a copy of any contract, license, or other document relating to this Agreement.

Copyright, Trademarks, and Other Proprietary Rights. Graphic Artist and Co-Graphic Artist agree that the Work shall be copyrighted in both their names, and that upon completion of the Work it is their intention that their respective contributions shall be merged into a joint work with a jointly owned copyright, unless provided to the contrary here: _____
_____. If either party does not complete their portion of the Work, the nature of copyright ownership shall be governed by Paragraph 3. It is further agreed that trademarks, rights in characters, titles, and similar ongoing rights shall be owned by both parties who shall both participate in any sequels under the terms of this Agreement, unless provided to the contrary here: _____. A sequel is defined as a work closely related to the Work in that it is derived from the subject matter of the Work, is similar in style and format to the Work, and is directed toward the same audience as that for the Work. Material of any and all kinds developed or obtained in the course of creating the work shall be [ ] jointly owned [ ] the property of the party who developed or obtained it.

Income and Expenses. Net proceeds generated by the Work shall be divided as set forth in this Paragraph. Net proceeds are defined as gross proceeds from the sale or license of book rights throughout the world (including but not limited to serializations, condensations, and translations), including advances, minus reasonable expenses. Such expenses shall include agents' fees and the parties' expenses incurred in the creation of the Work, provided that the parties' expenses shall be supported by appropriate verification and shall not exceed $_____ for the Graphic Artist and $_____ for the Co-Graphic Artist. Each party shall provide verification for expenses to the other party within 10 days of a written request. Unless otherwise provided, the parties' expenses shall be reimbursed from first proceeds received, including but not limited to advances.

Net proceeds from the sale or license of nonelectronic publishing rights shall be divided _____ percent to the Graphic Artist and _____ percent to the Co-Graphic Artist.

Net proceeds from the sale or license of electronic publishing rights shall be divided ____ percent to the Graphic Artist and ____ percent to the Co-Graphic Artist. For purposes of this agreement, electronic rights are defined as rights in the digitized form of works that can be encoded, stored, and retrieved from such media as computer disks, CD-ROMs, computer databases, and network servers.

Net proceeds from the sale or license of nonpublishing rights in the Work (including but not limited to audio, merchandising, motion picture, stage play, or television

rights to the Work), whether such sale or license occurs before or after initial publication of the Work, shall be divided _____ percent to the Graphic Artist and _____ percent to the Co-Graphic Artist, unless provided to the contrary here, in which case the following rights shall be treated with respect to division of net proceeds and control or disposition as follows: _____
_____
_____.

If possible, net proceeds shall be paid directly to each party in accordance with the divisions set forth in this Paragraph. If either party is designated to collect such net proceeds, that party shall make immediate payment to the other party of such amounts as are due hereunder.

Agent. If the parties have entered into an agency agreement with respect to the Work, it is with the following agent: _____. If a contract for the Work has not already been entered into with an agent, both Graphic Artist and Co-Graphic Artist agree [   ] to seek such a contract [   ] not to seek such a contract. Any agency contract shall be mutually acceptable to and entered into in the names of and signed by both the Graphic Artist and the Co-Graphic Artist, each of whom shall comply with and perform all required contractual obligations.

Graphic Artists Credit. The credit line for the Work shall be as follows wherever Graphic Artists credit is given in the Work or in promotion, advertising, or other ancillary uses: _____
The color and type size for such Graphic Artists credit shall be the same for both Graphic Artists unless provided to the contrary here: _____
_____.

Artistic Control. Each party shall have artistic control over his or her portion of the Work, unless provided to the contrary here in which case artistic control of the entire Work shall be exercised by _____. The parties shall share ideas and make their work in progress available to the other party for discussion and coordination purposes. Except as provided in Paragraphs 3 and 12, neither party shall at any time make any changes in the portion of the Work created by the other party.

Warranty and Indemnity. Graphic Artist and Co-Graphic Artist each warrant and represent to the other that the respective contributions of each to the Work are original (or that appropriate releases have been obtained and paid for) and do not libel or otherwise violate any right of any person or entity, including but not limited to rights of copyright or privacy. Graphic Artist and Co-Graphic Artist each indemnify and hold the other harmless from and against any and all claims, actions, liability, damages, costs, and expenses, including reasonable legal fees and expenses, incurred by the other as a result of the breach of such warranties, representations, and undertakings.

Assignment. This Agreement shall not be assignable by either party hereto, provided, however, that after completion of the Work, either party may assign the right to receive money pursuant to Paragraph 6 by giving written notice to the other party.

Death or Disability. In the event that either party dies or suffers a disability that will prevent completion of his or her respective portion of the Work, or of a revision thereof or a sequel thereto, the other party shall have the right to complete that portion or to hire a third party to complete that portion and shall adjust the Graphic Artists credit to reflect the revised Graphic Artists arrangements. The deceased or disabled party shall receive payments pursuant to Paragraph 6 pro rata to the proportion of his or her work completed or, in the case of a revision or sequel, shall receive payments pursuant to Paragraph 6 after deduction for the cost of revising or creating the sequel with respect to his or her portion of the Work. The active party shall have the sole power to license and contract with respect to the Work, and approval of the personal representative, heirs, or conservator of the deceased or disabled party shall not be required. If all parties are deceased, the respective heirs or personal representatives shall take the place of the parties for all purposes.

Arbitration. All disputes arising under this Agreement shall be submitted to binding arbitration before _____ in the following location _____ and shall be settled in accordance with the rules of the American Arbitration Association. Judgment upon the arbitration award may be entered in any court having jurisdiction thereof.

Term. The term for this Agreement shall be the duration of the copyright, plus any renewals or extensions thereof.

Independent Parties. The parties to this Agreement are independent of one another, and nothing contained in this Agreement shall make a partnership or joint venture between them.

Competitive Works. If the parties wish to restrict future activities to avoid competition with the Work, any such restrictions must be stated here: _____
_____
_____.

Infringement. In the event of an infringement of the Work, the Graphic Artist and Co-Graphic Artist shall have the right to sue jointly for the infringement and, after deducting the expenses of bringing suit, to share in any recovery as follows: _____ _____. If either party chooses not to join in the suit, the other party may proceed and, after deducting all the expenses of bringing the suit, any recovery shall be shared between the parties as stated in the preceding sentence.

Miscellany. This Agreement shall be binding upon the parties hereto, their heirs, successors, assigns, and personal representatives. This Agreement constitutes the entire understanding between the parties. Its terms can be modified only by an instrument in writing signed by both parties. Each party shall do all acts and sign all documents required to effectuate this Agreement. A waiver of any breach of any of the provisions of this Agreement shall not be construed as a continuing waiver of other breaches of the same or other provisions hereof. This Agreement shall be governed by the laws of the State of _____.

IN WITNESS WHEREOF, the parties hereto have signed this Agreement as of the date first set forth above.

Graphic Artist _____

Co-Graphic Artist _____

Joint Nondisclosure Agreement

This Joint Nondisclosure Agreement (hereinafter "JNDA") is entered into by and between _____ (hereinafter "Graphic Designer"), and _____ (hereinafter "Recipient" such designations being understood to include their subsidiaries or affiliates (collectively "the parties"). The effective date of this JNDA is _____, 20__.

The mutual objective of the parties hereto is to provide appropriate protection for Confidential Information (as defined herein) while maintaining our ability to conduct our respective business activities. Each of the parties wishes to enter into this JNDA to ensure that the terms and conditions hereof apply when one party ("Discloser") disclosed Confidential Information to the other ("Recipient") under this JNDA. NOW, THEREFORE, for good, valuable and binding consideration the receipt and sufficiency of which are hereby acknowledged, the parties hereto, intending to be legally bound hereby, agree as follows:

1. Definition of Confidential Information.

The term "Confidential Information" includes, among other things, all business strategies, formulae, notes, analyses, compilations, studies, interpretations or other documents prepared by Discloser or its representatives which contain, reflect or are based upon any information furnished to Recipient or its representatives pursuant hereto. The term "Confidential Information" does not include information which (i) is or becomes generally available to the public other than as a result of a disclosure by Recipient or its representatives, (ii) was rightfully within Recipient's possession prior to its being furnished by or on behalf of Discloser pursuant hereto or is disclosed to Recipient by another party without obligation of confidentiality, (iii) becomes available to Recipient on a non-confidential basis from a source other than the Discloser, or (iv) is developed independently by Recipient. Recipient's obligations shall only extend to Confidential Information that is clearly marked as confidential at the time disclosed or, if orally disclosed, is orally identified as confidential at the time disclosed. Confidential Information may be disclosed: (a) in writing; (b) by delivery of tangible things; (c) by initiation of access to information, such as may be contained in a computerized database; or (d) by oral and/or visual presentation.

2. Use of Confidential Information.

Recipient agrees that it will keep the Confidential Information confidential and use it solely for the purpose of evaluating a possible transaction between the Recipient and the Discloser.

3. Standard of Care.

Recipient agrees to use the same care and discretion to avoid disclosure, publication or dissemination of the Discloser's Confidential Information as it uses with its own similar information that it does not wish to disclose, publish or disseminate. Notwithstanding the foregoing, Recipient may (i) make any disclosure of such information to which Discloser gives its prior written consent, and (ii) disclose any such information to Recipient's representatives who need to know such information for the purpose of evaluating a possible transaction with Discloser and who agree for the benefit of Recipient and Discloser to keep such information strictly confidential.

4. Duration of Confidentiality Obligation.

Confidential Information disclosed pursuant to this JNDA will be subject to the terms of this JNDA for four years following the effective date hereof.

5. Nondisclosure of Relationship of Possible Transaction.

Each of the parties hereto agrees that, without the prior written consent of the other, it will not disclose to any person or entity the fact that Confidential Information has been made available hereunder, that discussions or negotiations are taking place concerning a possible transaction involving the parties hereto, or otherwise disclose any of the terms, conditions or other facts with respect hereto, including but not limited to the status thereof.

6. Mandatory Disclosure.

Notwithstanding any other provision hereof, in the event that Recipient is requested or required (by oral questions, interrogatories, requests for information or documents in legal proceedings, subpoena, civil investigative demand or other similar process) to disclose any of the Confidential Information, Recipient shall provide Discloser with prompt written notice of any such request or requirement so that Discloser may seek a protective order or other appropriate remedy. If, in the absence of a protective order or other remedy, Recipient is nonetheless legally compelled to disclose Confidential Information, Recipient may, without liability hereunder, disclose that portion of the Confidential Information which is legally required to be disclosed, provided that Recipient exercises reasonable efforts to preserve the confidentiality of the Confidential Information, including, without limitation, by cooperating with the Discloser to obtain an appropriate protective order or other reliable assurance that confidential treatment will be accorded the Confidential Information.

7. Return of Confidential Information.

If either party decides that it Graphic Design Companys not wish to proceed with a transaction with the other, it will promptly give notice of that decision in writing. In that case, or at any time upon the written request of the Discloser for any reason, Recipient will promptly deliver to Discloser all documents (and all copies thereof) furnished to Recipient by or on behalf of Discloser pursuant hereto. In the event of such decision or request, all other Confidential Information prepared by Discloser shall be destroyed and no copy thereof shall be retained. Notwithstanding the return or destruction of the Confidential Information, the parties hereto will continue to be bound by their obligations of confidentiality and other obligations hereunder.

8. No Representation.

Although the parties hereto have endeavored to include in the Confidential Information, information that they believe to be relevant for the purpose of the mutual evaluation of a possible transaction between the parties hereto, neither makes any representation or warranty as to the accuracy or completeness of the Confidential Information.

9. No License.

Neither this Agreement nor any disclosure of information hereunder grants the Recipient any right or license under any trademark, copyright, or patent now or hereafter owned or controlled by the Discloser.

10. No Restriction on Normal Business Activities.

So long as the Recipient complies with the terms hereof, the receipt of Confidential Information pursuant to this JNDA will not preclude the Recipient from providing to others products or services which may be competitive with products or services of the Discloser or providing products or services to others who compete with the Discloser.

11. Non-Competition.

Without the prior written consent of the other party, a party will not directly or indirectly solicit for employment any person employed by the other party or connected with the operation of its business for the following periods: if no transaction(s) between the parties result or develop, for a period of one (1) year from the effective date hereof; or, for a period of one (1) year after the conclusion of all business relations between the parties. Further, each party understands and agrees that all of the other party's employees have contractual obligations prohibiting them from entering into employment relationships with businesses that the other party at its sole discretion determines to be competitors.

12. General Provisions

    a. This JNDA does not require either party to disclose or to receive information or to enter into a transaction.

b. Neither party may assign, or otherwise transfer, its rights or delegate its duties or obligations under this JNDA without prior written consent of the other party. Any attempt to do so is void ab initio.

c. Recipient agrees to comply with all applicable laws, rules, and regulations relevant to the Confidential Information, including but not limited to government export and import laws and related regulations.

d. Either party may terminate this JNDA by providing ten (10) days' prior written notice to the other. The provisions of this JNDA, which, by their nature, extend beyond its termination, shall remain in full force and effect until fulfilled, and shall apply to respective successors and assignees.

e. No failure or delay by any party in exercising any right, power or privilege hereunder shall operate as a waiver thereof, nor shall any single or partial exercise thereof preclude any other or further exercise thereof or the exercise of any right, power or privilege hereunder.

f. It is further understood and agreed that money damages would not be a sufficient remedy for any breach of this JNDA and that the parties shall be entitled to equitable relief, including but not limited to injunction and specific performance, as a remedy for any such breach. Such remedies shall not be deemed to be the exclusive remedies for a breach of this JNDA but shall be in addition to all other remedies available at law or equity.

g. This JNDA shall be governed by and construed in accordance with the laws of the State of Pennsylvania, without giving effect to its conflict of laws, principles, or rules. Further, both parties consent to the jurisdiction of the state or federal courts located in Pennsylvania, with venue being proper in such jurisdiction.

h. This JNDA contains the entire agreement between the parties concerning the subject matter hereof and no modification or amendment of this JNDA or of the terms and conditions hereof will be binding upon either of the parties unless signed by both parties.

IN WITNESS WHEREOF, the Parties hereto have caused their duly authorized and empowered agents to execute this JNDA on and as of the date first hereinabove written.

By: _____   By: _____

Name: _____   Name: _____

Title: _____   Title: _____

Simple Letter for Nondisclosure

[Date]

[Name]
[Company]
[Address]
[City, State ZIP]

Dear _____:

This confirms our nondisclosure agreement:

1. Both of us agree that "confidential information" refers to any company-specific, or product/service-specific information provided to you by Graphic Design Company.

2. You agree to use reasonable care in safeguarding the security of our confidential [information].

3. You will not publish, copy, or disclose confidential information to any third party without prior written consent of Graphic Design Company.

4. You will use reasonable caution in preventing the inadvertent disclosure of Graphic Design Company information to [a third party.]

If you have any questions, please contact me. If you agree to this nondisclosure agreement, please acknowledge by signing this letter and returning to me. I look forward to working with you on our project..

Graphic Design Company   [name]

Signature _____   Signature _____

Date _____   Date _____

Appendix B
Graphic Designer Resources

They say you can never be rich enough or thin enough. While these could be argued, we believe you can never have enough resources. Therefore, we present for your consideration a wealth of sources for you to check into, check out, and harness for your own personal information blitz.

These sources are tidbits, ideas to get you started on your research. They are by no means the only sources out there and they should not be taken as the ultimate answer. We have done our research, but businesses do tend to move,

▲

change, fold, and expand. As we have repeatedly stressed, do your homework. Get out and start investigating.

Associations

Ad Council, 261 Madison Avenue, New York, NY 10016; (212) 922-1500, Fax (212) 922-1676; www.adcouncil.org

Advertising Photographers of America, PO Box 250, White Plains, NY 10605; (800) 272-6264, Fax (888) 889-7190; www.apanational.com

Advertising Photographers of New York (APNY), 27 West 20th Street, #601, New York, NY 10011; (212) 807-0399.

American Academy of Advertising, advertising.utexas.edu/AAA.

American Advertising Federation, 1101 Vermont Avenue NW, Suite 500, Washington, DC 20005-06306; (202) 898-0089 or (800) 999-2231, Fax: 202-898-0159; www.aaf.org

American Association of Advertising Agencies, 405 Lexington Avenue, New York, NY 10174-1801; (212) 682-2500; www.aaaa.org

American Association of Home Based Businesses, P.O. Box 10023, Rockville, MD 20849; (800) 447-9710, Fax: (301) 963-7042; www.aahbb.org

American Center for Design, 325 West Huron, Suite 711, Chicago, IL 60610; (312) 787-2018; www.ac4d.org

American Institute of Graphic Arts, 164 Fifth Avenue, New York, NY 10010; (212) 807-1990, Fax (212) 807-1799; www.aiga.org

American Marketing Association, 311 South Wacker Drive, Suite 5 (800), Chicago, IL 60606; (800) 262-1150, Fax (312) 542-9001; www.ama.org

American Society of Biz Publication Editors, 214 North Hale Street, Wheaton, IL 60187; (630) 510-4588, Fax 630-510-4501; www.asbpe.org

American Society of Business Publication Editors, 710 East Ogden Avenue #600, Naperville, IL 60563-8603; (630) 579-3288, Fax (630) 369-2488; E-mail: info@asbpe.org

American Society of Journalists and Authors, 1501 Broadway #302, New York, NY 10036; (212) 997-0947, Fax (212) 768-7414; www.asja.org

American Society of Media Photographers, 150 North Second Street, Philadelphia, PA 19106; (215) 451-2767, Fax (215) 451-0880; www.asmp.org

Art Directors and Artists Club, 2791 24th Street, Sacramento, CA 95818; (916) 731-8802, Fax (916) 731-4386; www.adac.org

Art Directors Club, 106 West 29th Street, New York, NY 10001; www.adcglobal.org

Artists In Print, 665 3rd Street, Suite 530, San Francisco, CA 94107; (415) 243-8244, (415) 362-1989; www.artistsinprint.org

Artists Rights Society, 536 Broadway, 5th Floor, (at Spring St.), New York, NY 10012; (212) 420-9160, Fax (212) 420-9286; www.arsny.com

Association for Information and Image Management (AIIM) International, 1100 Wayne Avenue, Suite 1100, Silver Spring, MD 20910; (301) 587 8202, Fax (301) 587 2711; www.aiim.org

Association for Multimedia Communications, P.O. Box 10645, Chicago, IL 60610; (312) 409-1032; www.amcomm.org

Association for Postal Commerce, 1901 N. Fort Myer Drive, Suite 401, Arlington, VA 22209-1609; (703) 524-0096, Fax (703) 524-1871; www.amma.org

Association for Women in Communications, 1244 Ritchie Highway, Suite 6, Arnold, MD 21012-1887; (410) 544-7442, Fax (410) 544-4640; www.womcom.org

Association of American Publishers, 71 Fifth Avenue, New York, NY 10003; (212) 255-0200, Fax (212) 255-7007; www.publishers.org

Association of Graphic Communications, 330 7th Avenue, New York, NY 10001; (212) 279-2116; www.agcomm.org.

Association of Internet Professionals, 9200 Sunset Boulevard, Suite 710, Los Angeles, CA 90069; (310) 724-6768, Fax (310) 724-6670; www.association.org

Association of Medical Illustrators, 1819 Peachtree Street NE, #560, Atlanta, GA 30309; (404) 350-7900, Fax (404) 351-3348; www.medical-illustrators.org

Audit Bureau of Circulations, 900 North Meacham Road, Schaumburg, IL 60173-4968; (847) 605-0909, Fax (847) 605-0483; www.accessabc.com

Authors Guild, 31 East 28th Street, 10th Floor, New York, NY 10016; (212) 563-5904; www.authorsguild.org

Brand Design Association, 164 5th Avenue New York, NY 10010; (212) 414-0296, Fax (212) 807-1799; www.branddesign.org

Broadcast Designers' Association, 145 West 45th Street, Suite 1100, New York, NY 10036; (212) 376-6222, Fax (212) 376-6202

▲

Business Marketing Association, 400 North Michigan Avenue, 15th Floor, Chicago, IL 60611; (800) 664-4262, Fax (312) 409-4266; www.marketing.org

Color Marketing Group, 5904 Richmond Highway, Suite 408, Alexandria, VA 22303; (703) 329-8500, Fax (703) 329-0155; www.colormarketing.org

Corporate Design Foundation, 20 Park Plaza, Suite 321, Boston, MA 02116; (617) 350-7097, Fax (617) 451-6355; www.cdf.org

Design Management Institute, 29 Temple Place, Boston, MA 02111-1350; (617) 338-6380, Fax (617) 338-6570; www.designmgt.org

Digital Printing & Imaging Association, 10015 Main Street, Fairfax, VA 22031; (703) 385-1339, Fax (703) 359-1336; www.dpia.org

Direct Marketing Association, 1120 Avenue of the Americas, New York, NY 10036-6700; (212) 768-7277, Fax (212) 302-6714; www.the-dma.org

Graphic Artists Guild, 90 John Street, Suite 403, New York, NY 10038-3202; (212) 791-3400, Fax (212) 791-0333; www.gag.org

Graphic Arts Show Company, Inc., 1899 Preston White Drive, Reston, VA 20191-4367; (703) 264-7200, Fax (703) 620-9187; www.gasc.org

Graphic Arts Technical Foundation (GATF), 200 Deer Run Road, Sewickley, PA 15143-2600; (800) 910-GATF, Fax (412) 741-2311; www.gatf.org

Graphic Arts Technical Foundation, 200 Deer Run Road, Sewickley, PA 15143-2600; (800) 910-GATF, Fax (412) 741-2311; www.gatf.org

Graphic Communications Association, 100 Daingerfield Road, Alexandria, VA 22314-2888; (703) 519-8160, Fax (703) 548-2867; www.gca.org

Greeting Card Association, 1350 New York Avenue NW, Suite 615, Washington, DC 20005; (202) 393-1778, Fax (202) 393-0336; www.greetingcard.org

Home Office Association of America, 133 East 58th Street, Suite 711, New York, NY 10022; (800) 809-4622, Fax (212) 588-9156

IAPHC (International Association of Printing House Craftsmen), 7042 Brooklyn Boulevard, Minneapolis, MN 55429-1370; (800) 466-4274 or (763) 560-1620, Fax (763) 560-1350; www.iaphc.org

International Interactive Communications Society (IICS), 39355 California Street, Suite 307, Fremont, CA 94538; (510) 608-5930, Fax (510) 608-5917; www.iics.org

International Prepress Association, 7200 France Avenue South, Suite 327, Edina, MN 55435; (612) 896-1908, Fax (612) 896-0181; www.ipa.org

International Publishing Management Association, 1205 West College Street, Liberty, MO 64068-3733; (816) 781-1111, Fax (816) 781-2790; www.ipma.org

IPA—The Association of Graphic Solutions Providers, 7200 France Avenue South, Suite 327, Edina, MN 55435; (952) 896-1908, Fax (952) 896-0181; www.ipa.org.

Magazine Publishers of America, 919 Third Avenue, New York, NY 10022; (212) 872-3700, Fax (212) 888-4217; www.magazine.org

National Association for Printing Leadership, 75 West Century Road, Paramus, NJ 07652; (800) 642-6275; www.napl.org

National Association of Photoshop Professionals (NAPP), 333 Douglas Road East, Oldsmar, FL 34677; (813) 433-5000, Fax (813) 433-5013; www.photoshopuser.com

National Association of Schools of Art and Design, 11250 Roger Bacon Drive, Suite 21, Reston, VA 20190-5248; nasad.arts-accredit.org

National Press Photographers Association, Inc., 3200 Croasdaile Drive, Suite 306, Durham, NC 27705; (919) 383-7246, Fax (919) 383-7261; www.nppa.org

National Writers Union, 113 University Place, 6th Floor, New York, NY 10003; (212) 254-0279; www.nwu.org

New York New Media Association, 55 Broad Street, 3rd Floor, New York, NY 10004; (212) 785-7898, Fax (212) 785-7963; www.nynma.org

NPES, 1899 Preston White Drive, Reston, VA 20191-4367; (703) 264-7200, Fax (703) 620-0994; www.npes.org

Organization of Black Designers, 300 M Street SW, Suite N110, Washington, DC 20024-4019; (202) 659-3918; www.core77.com/OBD

Pacific Printing and Imaging Association, 5319 S.W. Westgate Drive, Suite 117, Portland, OR 97221-2430; (877) 762-7742, Fax: (503) 297-3320; www.ppi-assoc.org

Photo Marketing Association International, 3000 Picture Place, Jackson, MI 49201; www.pmai.org

Professional Photographers of America, Inc., 229 Peachtree Street, NE, #2200, Atlanta, GA 30303-2206; (404) 522-8600, Fax (404) 614-6400; www.ppa.com

Professional Photographers' Society of New York, Inc., 706 Quaker Lane, Delanson, NY 12053; (518) 895-2460, Fax (518) 895-2329; www.ppsny.com

Promotion Marketing Association, Inc., 257 Park Avenue South, 11th Floor, New York, NY 10010; (212) 420-1100, Fax: (212) 533-7622; www.pmalink.org

Society for Environmental Graphic Design (SEGD), 401 F Street NW, Suite 333, Washington, DC 20001; (202) 638-5555, Fax: (202) 638-0891; www.segd.org

▲

Society for Imaging Science and Technology, 7003 Kilworth Lane, Springfield, VA 22151; (703) 642-9090; www.imaging.org

Society of Illustrators, 128 East 63rd Street, New York, NY 10021; (212) 838-2560, Fax (212) 838-2561; www.societyillustrators.org

Society of Photographer and Artist Reps (SPAR), 60 East 42nd Street, Suite 1166, New York, NY 10165; (212) 779-7464

Society of Professional Journalists, 3909 North Meridian Street, Indianapolis, IN 46208; (317) 927-8000; www.spj.org

Society of Publication Designers, 17 East 47th Street, 6th Floor, New York, NY 10017; (212) 223-3332, Fax (212) 223-5880; www.spd.org

Society of Publication Designers, 60 East 42nd Street, Suite 721, New York, NY 10165; (212) 983-8585, Fax (212) 983-6043

Specialized Information Publishers Association, 8201 Greensboro Drive, Suite 300, McLean, VA 22102; (703) 610-0260 or (800) 356-9302, Fax (703) 610-9005; www.sipaonline.org

Triangle Production Association, P.O. Box 31441, Raleigh, NC 27622-1441; www.nctpa.org

Type Directors Club, 60 East 42nd Street, Suite 721, New York, NY 10165; (212) 983-6042, Fax (212) 938-6043; www.tdc.org/indexfr.htm

University and College Designers Association, 122 South Michigan Avenue, Suite 1100, Chicago, IL 60603; (312) 431-0013, Fax (312) 431-8697; www.ucda.com

Books

Crawford, Tad, and Eva Doman Bruck. *Business and Legal Forms for Graphic Designers, 3rd Edition*, Allworth Press, 2003

Crawford, Tad. *The Graphic Design Business Book*, Allworth Press, 2005

Foote, Cameron S. *The Creative Business Guide to Running a Graphic Design Business*, W. W. Norton & Company, 2004

Shaughnessy, Adrian, and Stefan Sagmeister. *How to Be a Graphic Designer without Losing Your Soul*, Princeton Architectural Press, 2005

Williams, Theo Stephan. *Graphic Designer's Guide to Pricing, Estimating & Budgeting Revised Edition*, Allworth Press, 2001

Magazines

GRAPHIC DESIGN USA, 79 Madison Avenue, Suite 1202, New York, NY 10016; (212) 696-4380, Fax (212) 696-4564; www.gdusa.com

HOW magazine, 4700 East Galbraith Road, Cincinnati, OH 45236; www.howdesign.com

PRINT Magazine, PO Box 420235, Palm Coast, FL 32142-0235; (877) 860-9145; www.printmag.com

Mailing List Provider

Chessie Lists, 13321 New Hampshire Avenue, Suite 202, Silver Spring, MD 20904; (301) 680-3633, Fax (301) 680-3635; www.chessielists.com

Useful Web Sites

All Graphic Design, www.allgraphicdesign.com

Alliance for Affordable Services, www.affordableservices.com

Cartoon Syndicate, www.unitedmedia.com or www.kingfeatures.com

Degrees-for-Success, Degrees-for-success.com

Design Talk Board, www.designtalkboard.com

Digital Thread, www.digitalthread.com

Direct mail information, www.uspsdirectmail.com

Freelance Designers, www.freelancedesigners.com

U.S. Copyright Office, www.loc.gov/copyright

U.S. Postal Service, www.usps.com

Web developers resource, www.webmonkey.com

Glossary

Acrobat: A part of a set of applications developed by Adobe to create and view PDF files.

Active server page: A dynamically generated web page, generally using ActiveX scripting.

Aliasing: A condition that occurs when a computer monitor, printer, or graphics file does not have a high enough resolution to represent a graphic image or text.

Alignment: The positioning of a body of text. Text can be positioned to the left, right, or "center" of a page.

Animated GIF: A GIF graphic file, which consists of two or more images shown in a timed sequence to give the effect of motion.

Animation: Animation is the creation of a timed sequence or series of graphic images or frames together to give the appearance of continuous movement.

Anti-aliasing: Smoothing or blending the transition of pixels in an image.

ASP: See Active Server Page.

C1S: Abbreviation for coated one side.

▲

C2S: Coated two sides.

Camera-ready copy: Mechanicals, photographs, and art fully prepared for reproduction according to the technical requirements of the printing process being used.

Case: Covers and spine that, as a unit, enclose the pages of a casebound book.

CD/R: Compact Disc/Recordable is a compact disc that is a Write Once, Read Many optical medium.

CMYK: Abbreviation for cyan, magenta, yellow, and key (black), the four process colors.

Coarse screen: Halftone screen with ruling of 65, 85, or 100 lines per inch (26, 34 or 40 lines per centimeter).

Collate: To organize printed matter in a specific order as requested.

Color balance: Refers to amounts of process colors that simulate the colors of the original scene or photograph.

Color correct: To adjust the relationship among the process colors to achieve desirable colors.

Commercial printer: Printer producing a wide range of products such as announcements, brochures, posters, booklets, stationery, business forms, books, and magazines. Sometimes also called a job printer, because each job is different.

Composition: The arrangement of type, graphics, and other elements on the page.

Crop marks: Lines near the edges of an image indicating portions to be reproduced.

CWT: Abbreviation for hundredweight using the Roman numeral C.

Cyan: One of the four process colors. Also known as process blue.

Database: A structured collection of records or data that is stored in a computer system.

Dedicated line: A dedicated line is a permanent connection to the internet using an individual, separate phone line.

Desktop publishing: Technique of using a personal computer to design images and pages, and assemble type and graphics, then using a laser printer or imagesetter to output the assembled pages onto paper, film, or printing plate.

DHTML: Dynamic Hypertext Mark-up Language that is an HTML extension that allows web pages to react to the end users' input, such as displaying a web page based on the type of browser or computer end users are viewing a page with.

Die: Device for cutting, scoring, stamping, embossing, and debossing.

Digital proofing: Page proofs produced through electronic memory transferred onto paper via laser or ink-jet.

DNS: Domain Name System that translates URL text addresses (such as gdesigns.com) into a numeric internet address (such as 202.212.181.106).

Double density: A method of recording electronically (disk, CD, floppy) using a modified frequency to allow more data storage.

DPI: Considered as "dots per square inch," a measure of output resolution in relationship to printers, imagesetters, and monitors.

Drop shadow: A drop shadow gives an image depth by creating a shading offset behind a selected image.

DTP: See desktop publishing

Dummy: Simulation of the final product. Also called mockup.

English finish: Smooth finish on uncoated book paper; smoother than eggshell, rougher than smooth.

EPS: Encapsulated Post Script, a known file format usually used to transfer post script information from one program to another.

Fine screen: Screen with ruling of 150 lines per inch (80 lines per centimeter) or more.

Fixed costs: Costs that remain the same regardless of how many pieces are printed. Copyrighting, photography, and design are fixed costs.

Folio: The page number.

Format: Size, style, shape, layout, or organization of a layout or printed product.

Galley: Page proofs from the commercial printer.

GIF: Graphics Interchange Format. GIF images display up to 256 colors and are the most widely.

Gigabyte: A unit of computer memory or storage; often called gigs. A gigabyte is one billion bytes.

Glow: A glow is the opposite of a shadow in that it creates a surrounding highlight of an image.

Gradient: A gradual transition of colors.

Graphic backgrounds: The bottom layer on a web page, usually with either a design or color that highlights the copy above.

Grayscale: An application of black ink (for print) or the color black (for the screen) that simulates a range of tones. Grayscale images have no hue (color).

GUI: Graphical user interface.

Gutter: Interior margin of the book that is bound.

Hairline: Very thin rule.

High resolution: A bitmap image that has a high pixel resolution.

Pantone matching system: A registered trade name for a system of numbered ink colors.

PDF: The Portable Document Format is the computer file format created and controlled by Adobe Systems for document exchange.

PPI: Pixels per inch.

Print on demand: The process of printing a book when it is ordered. Each page is printed individually, rather than with a signature.

RGB: Red-Green-Blue.

Rich media: Web site or banner ads that use technology more advanced than standard GIF animation.

Rivers: A typographic term for the ugly white gaps that occur in justified columns of type when there is too much space between the words.

Royalty-free: Photos, graphic images, or other intellectual property that are sold for a single standard fee and may be used repeatedly by the purchaser.

Signature: A large sheet of printed pages, which when folded and cut, become a part of a book or publication.

Thumbnail: A small version of a graphic image.

TIFF: Tag image file format.

Work for hire: Material produced under a written agreement by a freelancer where all rights have been assigned to the publisher.

WYSIWYG: Abbreviation for What You See Is What You Get.

XHTML: Abbreviation for Extensible Hypertext Mark-up Language and is a hybrid of XML and HTML.

XML: Abbreviation for Extensible Mark-up Language.

Index